THE ROGUE I REMEMBER

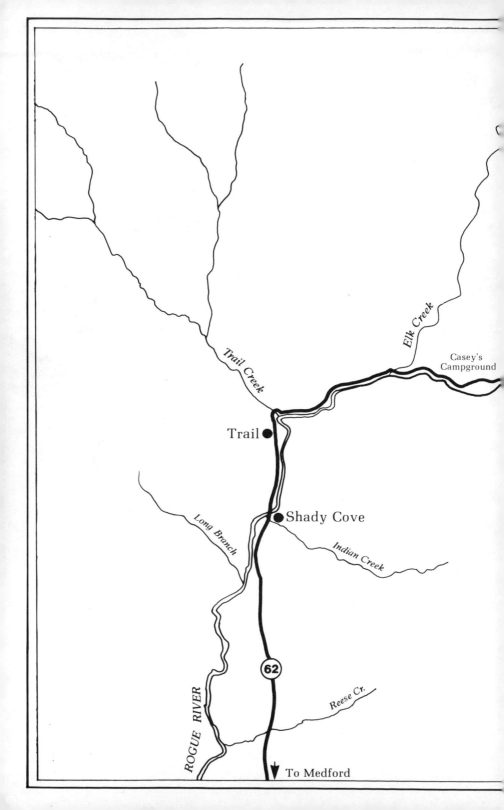

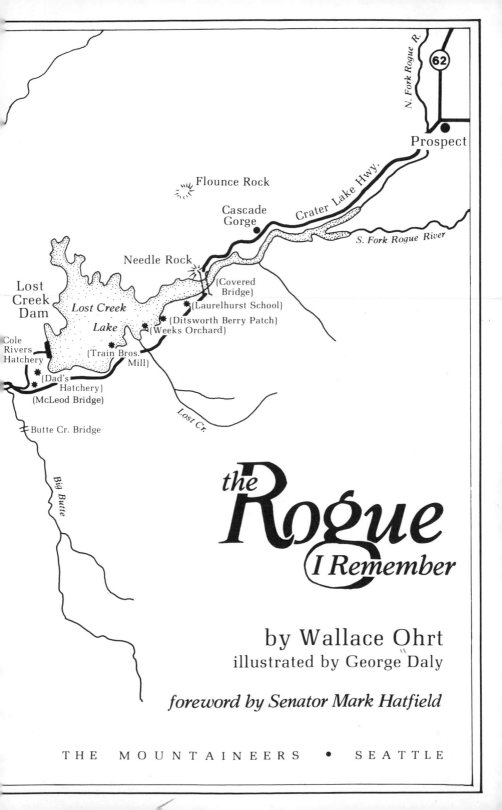

the Rogue
I Remember

by Wallace Ohrt
illustrated by George Daly

foreword by Senator Mark Hatfield

THE MOUNTAINEERS • SEATTLE

The Mountaineers
Organized 1906
To explore and study the mountains, forests, and watercourses of the Northwest;
To gather into permanent form the history and traditions of this region;
To preserve by the encouragement of protective legislation or otherwise the
  natural beauty of Northwest America;
To make expeditions into these regions in fulfillment of the above purposes;
To encourage a spirit of good fellowship among all lovers of outdoor life.

Published by
The Mountaineers
719 Pike Street
Seattle, Washington 98101

Manufactured in the United States of America

Edited by Rebecca Earnest
Design by Eleanor Mathews

Library of Congress Cataloging in Publication Data

Ohrt, Wallace L
    The Rogue I remember.

    1. Ohrt, Wallace L. 2. Rogue River Valley, Or. — Social life and
customs. 3. Rogue River Valley, Or. — Biography. I. Title.
F882.R60476   979.5'21   79-17166
ISBN 0-916890-94-5

dedication

To John Franklin Ditsworth, born at Eagle Point, Oregon, July 2, 1881, died at Medford, Oregon, October 31, 1978, I gratefully and affectionately dedicate this book.

The echoes fade, the shadows fall,
The river's roar is still.
No panther prowls the forest hall,
No coyote howls on the hill.

Farewell, then, O settler's son,
This land has known your best;
The harvest's in, your work is done;
It's time for you to rest.

The paths are dim, the great trees gone,
The strawberry rows lie plundered;
And pastures green like rolling lawn
Are now six fathoms under.

In winter's drifts and summer's toil,
As rancher and leader of men,
You left your print on Oregon soil,
And we'll not see your like again.

— WLO

contents

foreword

WALLACE L. OHRT, in his book *The Rogue I Remember*, offers a nostalgic visit to life in the Upper Rogue River Valley during the period 1927-1937. Although that time and place are now gone forever, the reader experiences them through the eyes of those who were there. Unlike most nostalgic looks at the past, Mr. Ohrt effectively portrays life in a bygone era without directly attacking the present. In an unbiased manner he juxtaposes life during the Depression years and that of today. This contrast highlights profound changes, not only in the physical area of the Upper Rogue River Valley, but in the attitudes and values held by the people of the two respective eras. There are changes in male-female roles, changes in people's expectations of the federal government and their perception of how our natural resources should be utilized, and even changes in the structure of worship in the rural Christian church.

Life during the Depression in the Upper Rogue River Valley was characterized by rugged self-reliance. Isolated from the mainstream of society, the inhabitants were forced to fend for themselves against the elements. Separation from city life and the absence of "big government" made self-reliance for those in the Upper Rogue River Valley a necessity, not a choice. Stemming from this self-reliance was the ideal of the self-made man. Men dreamed big dreams. Everyone longed for the life of the entrepreneur, the life of the self-made man.

The loneliness inherent to isolation, while a burden in many ways, was a boon to family life. In the 1930s, individual family units were sprinkled throughout the Upper Rogue Valley and often were separated by several miles. This isolation from others forced children and parents alike to seek fulfillment from within the family. Parents spent time with their children; brothers and sisters played together instead of with friends from the neighborhood. "Visiting" was a major occasion, since families had to travel great distances to spend time with their "neighbors."

The Rogue I Remember is a valuable addition to the historical record of Oregon. By outlining the early settlement of the Upper Rogue River area, Mr. Ohrt succeeds in raising several questions about the desirability of "progress": Has the shift from rural to urban living, and the increasing involvement of government in daily life, sapped the citizenry of its desire for or its ability to maintain individualism? Have affluence and careerism undermined traditional family values? Is there hope for the preservation of our wilderness and natural resources as long as the materialistic urge to consume remains so strong? These questions arise, not becuase Mr. Ohrt attacks present day urban life, big government, affluence, careerism, or consumerism, but because he paints a truly delightful picture of the past — a past that provides a useful context for reflection upon our current problems and the critical decisions that lie ahead.

—Senator Mark O. Hatfield
Washington, D.C.
August 20, 1979

preface

SOME OF MY FRIENDS have been puzzled about my reasons for
writing this book. Their questions carry overtones of skepticism,
for the remote and isolated segment of the Upper Rogue River
Valley in southern Oregon that is the real "hero" of this account
is — I should say was — of no particular significance to anyone
who has never been there.

I must get used to speaking of this cherished place in the past
tense, for, as my story relates, it has been relegated to oblivion
and is now slowly filling with water behind a 360-foot-high
federal dam. The reasons for constructing the dam seem irre-
proachable: It will protect the more populous lower valley from
destructive winter floods, provide water for the irrigation of
crops, and entertain future generations of water-sport lovers, not
to mention the many jobs and contracts it will create in the
process. Only an ungrateful curmudgeon would oppose such a
cornucopia of benefits. Who can argue?

But my comments concerning the dam project are incidental
to the main purpose behind this book. I wrote it for the same
reason that I narrated the incidents described therein so many
times to my children at bedtime: for the simple pleasure of
remembering, and sharing with them, the joys and tribulations
of a way of life that seems as remote as the moon from today's
increasingly structured existence. And incidentally to record
that beneath the waters of that imposing dam there was a place
where people I knew and loved once struggled against the Great
Depression, where wild animals roamed in the woods and flowers bloomed in the springtime.

Among those who have reviewed this book, some were trou-
bled by what they term "the frontier approach to uses of the
environment." Why, they ask, such a distressing slaughter of
game and shooting of predators? I understand the basis for the
question and find it both challenging and disturbing, for it goes
to the heart of what I am trying to say. If I fail in this, I have failed
altogether.

In this book I propose to visit the Upper Rogue River in southern Oregon during the period 1927-1937. The time and the place are now gone forever. The reader can experience them only through the eyes of those who were there; and we, of course, did not then have the attitudes, standards, and perceptions that prevail today.

With reference to our "uses of the environment," one must differentiate between the actions of adults and those of juveniles. The grown-ups were much too busy battling the Depression to engage in casual despoliation of nature, which was not always the case with us youngsters. When we shot salmon in Big Butte Creek or rolled boulders over cliffs, we did it for the sheer mindless thrill of it, just as today's kids rip up the landscape and squander fuel in their cars and motorcycles. Our parents, like parents of today, frowned on such wanton follies but were not always able to prevent them. Men poached deer and salmon in those days for the simple reason that they had no money to buy meat and were philosophically opposed to starvation. Water, timber, land, scenery, and other natural resources were considered inexhaustible. "Environment" was not a common word in our vocabulary, and you could have stumped a college professor with "ecology." "Conservation," on the other hand, was a familiar and respectable term; we knew a lot about conserving.

The notion that any of the wild creatures that abounded around us might be threatened with extinction would have seemed far-fetched, and the conventional wisdom of that day would have declared that extinction was too good for some of them. Until his death last November at age ninety-seven, my dear old pioneer friend Frank Ditsworth never wavered in his conviction that one of man's greatest mistakes was his failure to exterminate the coyote when the opportunity presented itself. If, now that he is gone, I should attempt to create sympathy for Frank by presenting him as a friend of the wily varmint that eluded his traps for sixty or so years, I should, in so doing, falsify my own purposes as well as his reputation.

Furthermore, he would undoubtedly look down pityingly at me, shake his head, and exclaim, "The dang fool's gone soft in the head. Been livin' in the city too long!"

acknowledgments

IN REACHING BACK more than half a century to record bygone events, one inevitably incurs a debt to other people who have lived longer — and remember more — than he does. My mother, currently writing her own recollections of her eventful eighty-seven years, shared her notes and memories with me. Mrs. Frances Pearson, who was my Prospect High School history and English teacher, and who from birth lived nearly all of her ninety-three years in that quaint mountain settlement, contributed much of the material for chapter ten, as well as other passages. Maude Ditsworth crossed the Siskiyou Mountains into the Rogue River Valley in her father's wagon when she was seven and later became almost a second mother to the Laurelhurst kids; her store of loving memories helped write these pages. And how can I thank Frank Ditsworth — Maude's beloved "Frankie" — now gone after living nearly a century in the Rogue country? I had hoped to present him with a copy of this book, which could not have been written without his help.

To these four stalwart old-timers, whose lives exemplify the best of our pioneer past — honesty, simplicity, courage, self-reliance, and hard work — I give my thanks.

In addition, there are many friends whose support I deeply appreciate. Dave Becker was the first to speak a professional word of encouragement. Ken Bushnell served cheerfully as unpaid agent. Alex Lamon drew on a lifetime of publishing experience to help a greenhorn friend. And Amos Wood, who has encouraged a host of aspiring Northwest writers, persuaded me to expose my manuscript to some piercing and highly perceptive criticisms. To all of these I owe a deep and enduring debt of gratitude.

chapter one
The Rogue

THE NORTH FORK of the Rogue rises out of a cluster of springs on the western flank of the Oregon Cascades ten miles or so to the north of that great natural fantasy, Crater Lake. Winding southerly, the North Fork is joined in the depths of Cascade Gorge by the combined Middle and South forks. Downstream a few miles, the river, swinging west, emerges onto a somewhat broader but still rugged valley. Here, the north bank was once threaded by the tortuous and scenic Crater Lake Highway. To the south, across the river, a bench of land once nestled below the Rogue River Mountains, a short spur of the Cascade Range. This bench-land for a time formed a remote and thinly populated district that had come to be known as Laurelhurst.

The inhabitants of this community maintained contact with the outside world by means of a narrow, shale-surfaced road called Laurelhurst Loop. At the southern, or downstream, end of this road, the McLeod bridge spanned a rocky, high-walled channel; for nearly half a mile upstream the road hugged the face of a cliff. Opening onto easier terrain, the little road then wound for five or six miles through a height of land above the river, eventually recrossing the Rogue by a picturesque covered bridge and rejoining the Crater Lake Highway at Flounce Rock.

My family discovered this secluded corner of southern Oregon during the summer of my sixth year. Dad had found an undeveloped campground just where the road emerged from the cliff face, and here he liked to come to fish for trout and steelhead. On arrival we would all pile out of the old Stevens touring car and Dad would carefully fit together the sections of his handmade rod. Mom unloaded the picnic supplies and my two brothers and I struck off on some tour of exploration. There were thickets and ravines nearby and — though the swift current of the Rogue denied us entry to it — a brush-choked island set like a crescent in the river bend below us.

Dad's considerable skills did not include the cunning demanded of a steelheader, so he usually abandoned this pursuit in disgust after a couple of hours. But he would delay the thirty-mile drive back to Medford as long as possible, usually lounging in the shade of the tall firs on an old canvas tarpaulin. He never tired of listening to the scolding jays or watching an insouciant silver-gray squirrel, tail aflirt, as it raced along the old moss-covered snake fence.

Mom was in no greater hurry than Dad to return to the heat of the lower valley. At the time, she was recovering slowly from a physical and emotional breakdown — the doctor called it a stroke of paralysis — brought on by overwork. For four years she had been caring for five self-centered males: her three toddling sons, her brilliant but often remote and distracted husband, and

Dad's ailing, nearly blind father. The poor old man had finally succumbed, just before Mom collapsed, and it was this deliverance from responsibility for him that had made these outings possible.

But her health was still precarious. Dr. Howard had told her that she might not get all of her strength back for as long as ten years. This she had withheld from Dad, who was solicitous enough but baffled and ill at ease in the presence of sickness. He always spoke disparagingly of any discussion of personal symptoms as an "organ recital" and kept his own physical problems strictly to himself.

Mom was of much the same mold as Dad. Her resolute character and spartan Norwegian background forbade her the solace of talking about her troubles, so she simply struggled on one day at a time, trusting that she would somehow find the energy her duties required. In this sylvan setting, the roar of the river and the feel of the sunlight filtering through the tall firs were, to her thinking, better than any medicine.

So together they idled away the Sunday afternoons, Dad occasionally sharing aloud his expansive visions and Mom responding absent-mindedly, conscious only of the release from care and trusting her husband to bring the family to better days. We boys found plenty to do, little knowing what a radical change was soon to enter our lives.

MY FATHER was a native of Iowa. He and my mother met and married in Moose Jaw, Saskatchewan, in 1915. After Danny and I were born, a small legacy from his grandmother offered an escape from the bitter prairie winters, of which both Mom and Dad had had enough. They decided to take a vacation in California and then move to a place with a mild climate year-round. It was October 1919 when we headed south; Danny was nearing two and I was about five months old.

As our California-bound train roared through the Siskiyou foothills of Oregon, our parents were astonished to see a group of boys swimming in the nude not far from the tracks — the weather had long since turned icy back home. They were sufficiently impressed to return after vacation and establish a home in Medford. Only then did they learn that the swimmers had been enjoying a late October plunge in the now-famous Jackson Hot Springs near Ashland!

At the time my story begins, we had lived about five years in a moderately imposing house of California mission architecture, a style that had taken Dad's fancy on the vacation trip. It was of H-shaped design with stucco siding and a simulated red tile roof. It was considered rather grand for its time. Surrounding us were pear orchards, alfalfa fields, and a pickle factory.

Across the street stood the only other house on that newly established block, the old Marshall place. The Marshalls had two sons, Vern and Edison. Vern was about Dad's age and considered normal, but Edison had literary aspirations and was therefore considered odd. Today, after making a place for himself as one of America's most popular and prolific novelists (*The Voice of the Pack,* 1920; *Benjamin Blake,* 1941; *The Vikings,* 1951; *The Lost Colony,* 1964; etc.) he is regarded more favorably by his old neighbors.

Our life in Medford, aside from our mother's overwork, was not altogether lacking in elegance. Following Mom's stroke, we briefly enjoyed that vanishing status symbol, a maid living in. And there was a garden party or two, with Japanese lanterns swinging from the walnut trees in the front yard.

There were always dogs around our place in those years. Dad's interest in the breeding, training, and sale of Chesapeake Bay retrievers dated back to his life in Saskatchewan, where he had enjoyed some of the finest waterfowl hunting to be found anywhere in the world. To his delight, the same fabulous shooting existed in the Klamath Basin, some sixty miles east of Medford. With the encouragement of his hunting companions, he launched the Rogue Valley Chesapeake Kennels as an avocation in about 1921. Soon Danny and I, and later Bobby, were toddling fearlessly among these large, powerful canine companions, whom we accepted as a natural part of our environment.

Other memories of Medford come flooding back to me. Warm spring days brought forth oceans of yellow mustard blossoms in the neighboring vacant lots, and waxy California poppies sprouted along the sidewalks. The Ringling Brothers circus came, with all the fascinating paraphernalia of the "big top." Downtown, the smoky door of the blacksmith shop yawned. I would often forget the errand on which I had been sent while I watched the sweating smith in his leather apron and listened to the impatient stamping of the horses.

But on those Sunday afternoons on the Upper Rogue, as the sun dipped behind the ridges, Medford seemed a distant and altogether unappealing place. Our parents would begin to stir themselves, folding and packing, while we did our best to extend our leave.

Staring out across the willow-bordered meadow by the river, Dad would say, "Sig, doesn't that look like a good place for a fish hatchery?"

"Of course, Norm," she would agree. Then we would climb into the Stevens and head for home, a full hour away by Dad's cautious driving.

chapter two
Dad makes the move

OUR PICNICS on the Upper Rogue became regular weekend
events. Dad was spending less time trying to catch steelhead and
more tramping the rolling hills and river bottom land. The idea
of starting a fish hatchery had formed in his mind after taking us
to a trout farm some months previously, and it was by now
becoming an obsession. The abandoned farm adjacent to our
campground appealed powerfully to his imagination as a site for
such an enterprise. The large meadow by the river seemed ideal

6

for his rearing ponds, and he saw other intriguing features about the property.

Quite near the campground, for example, there was an old apple orchard of thirty or so trees, overage and unpruned but still bearing fruit. Close to the orchard was a series of fine springs with a good flow of clear, cold water, and at the site of the vanished dwelling were two large cherry trees and an immense fir. All that remained of the house itself were a stone chimney and some concrete foundation piers, but two serviceable log barns stood nearby, one of them surrounded by a sturdy pole corral.

Dad investigated at the county courthouse in Jacksonville and tracked down the owner of this phantom property, an elderly widower named Charles Toney who was living alone in a small house near Medford. A wistful gleam came into the old man's eye when Dad mentioned the purpose of his visit.

"So ye heard about it, did ye, mister?" His voice was as thin and dry as a corn husk. "Well, it's all still there, waitin' for the right man to come an' git it. But that ain't me no more, I reckon."

"What's there, Mr. Toney?" Dad asked, puzzled.

The bushy brows drew together and the dry voice fell to a conspiratorial whisper. "Why, gold, man, gold! Ain't that what you're after? You must 'a seen my diggin's there in the yard!"

Dad nodded. "I saw a dry hole covered with boards. I thought it was a well."

The old man snorted. "No need to dig a well through solid rock. There's sweet water from the spring on the edge of the orchard, right at the surface. No, siree; that ain't no well. That's a treasure hole, an' some lucky cuss is gonna stick his pick into solid gold right there someday!"

"If you're so sure of that, why aren't you still working it?" Dad asked.

The dry lips quivered and the Adam's apple bobbed with agitation.

"Old age and rheumatiz caught up with me. Couldn't git no help out'n them boys o' mine. Finally they took off an' left me. I kep' workin' it on the good days, when my rheumatiz wasn't too bad. Then one day a spark from the chimney lit on the cedar roof. Dry, hot day, it was. No water pressure from them springs, nothin' but a bucket an' a busted ladder. Finally the fire got away from me an' I just give up. Got my gear out'n the house, all I could before the roof fell in, then I just stood there under the cherry tree an' watched her burn."

Dad was silent for a time. Then he asked, "How did you get the idea there is gold there? Did you ever find any?"

Old Charley Toney shook his grizzled head. "I bought the place about twenty years ago off Jeff Brophy, the man who proved it up. He was runnin' goats there, but he decided to sell out an' move to another place he had a couple miles upriver. I made a trip to Frisco for supplies an' while I was there I found out for certain I had a gold mine on my hands."

"How could you learn in San Francisco that a property in southern Oregon had gold on it?"

"I come out of a saddle shop an' noticed a sign that said, Unlock the Secrets of Your Life. I went in an' seen a black-haired woman sitting there in the dark, like. Awful purty woman, she was. She motioned me to sit down an' she looked at my hands an' at some cards.

"Finally, she tells me that I have just taken a step that will make me rich if I am willing to work hard. She said, 'I see a large oak tree with wide, spreading branches. Under the branches, on the south side of the tree, there is much gold in the ground. It will not be easy to find, but in the end you will be richly rewarded. You will be a very wealthy man.' "

Dad stared incredulously at the old man. "You mean that you spent twenty years digging through solid rock on a fortune teller's say-so?"

"Eighteen years," Toney corrected him. "Eighteen hard years, not countin' time out to earn money for grub an' tools an' dynamite. But my wife died an' my kids didn't have no faith. One by one, they growed up an' moved out. Then the fire an' the goddam rheumatiz finished me." His eyes were dim and lusterless and his dry voice very low. "But it's still there, mister, an' it's yours if you got the grit to go after it."

Discussions with Charley Toney continued, though Dad was never able to convince the old man that gold was not his inducement. He was delighted to learn that the property encompassed 205 acres, including a full mile of Rogue River frontage terminating downstream at our campground. All of this Charles Toney was willing to sell for three thousand dollars: a considerable sum in those days, but Dad was confident that the equity in the Medford house, plus the residue of his inheritance, would enable him to purchase the land and all the necessary equipment.

The only remaining problem was to persuade Mom of the feasibility of the project, and this proved less difficult than Dad had anticipated. She was already strongly attracted to the river locale, and as she listened to Dad expound his idea she began to share his vision. Much later she concluded that there were five compelling reasons that enabled them to reach their decision.

First, Mom sensed with something like desperation that she must escape her present environment if she was ever to recover her health. The hot Medford summers drained her energy, and the house on South Holly had come to be associated with illness, death, and defeat. Second, Dad, too, was having health problems: The fumes from his oxyacetylene welding business were proving highly toxic, and the noise from an adjacent body and fender shop was affecting his hearing. Third, both felt certain that the country would be a more wholesome place for the raising of their three sons. Fourth, Dad's dream of the trout farm had so gripped both their imaginations that, emotionally, they had passed the point of turning back from this objective. And finally, the opportunity to fish, hunt, and otherwise "live off the land" appealed strongly to their pioneer spirit.

Having settled the matter and negotiated an agreement, Dad moved swiftly. He knew all about striking while the iron is hot. Within a few weeks he had sold the Vulcan Welding Works, taken a second mortgage on our Medford house, and rounded up a crew to work with him on the construction of our riverside home. Although winter was due to set in soon, he erected a tent-house near the building site and cooked his meals by campfire while the job was in progress. The architectural style of our new home, he informed Mom upon his departure, was to be Swiss chalet, in keeping with the mountain setting. We saw little of him for the next few months.

He met an elderly farmer named Carl Richardson who turned out to be skilled in stone masonry, so Dad put him in charge of constructing a basement of fieldstones. A journeyman carpenter worked with Dad on the frame structure, and two hard-looking drifters were engaged as general handymen. These two, later identified as escaped convicts, hauled stones and nailed floor-ing, all the while carrying heavy six-shooters strapped to their thighs. They always kept a sharp lookout toward the road and took their meals apart from Dad's camp. One evening a shot rang out from the direction of their campfire, and Dad rushed over to find one man clutching his right calf. He had shot himself while cleaning his revolver — or so they explained it to Dad. Soon after that the two hoboes collected their pay and cleared camp.

"YOU CALL THIS a Swiss chalet?" Mom demanded when Dad showed us the completed dwelling.

Dad grinned. "Can't you hear the yodelers up there on the mountainside?"

To my brothers and me, architectural authenticity seemed unimportant. The quaint little dwelling and its rustic setting were a new and enchanting world. The house overlooked the Rogue River from a sidehill location set back about a quarter-mile from the stream and perhaps seventy feet above its banks. It was certainly different from any house we had ever seen. Of simple shed roof structure, it lay parallel to the hillside, on a terracelike level area midway up a moderately steep slope. Viewed from the front, it seemed low and unpretentious, but from the downhill side its stone foundation loomed impres-sively.

As we entered the lower level to begin our inspection of the interior, Mom stared in dismay. "Why isn't there a floor?" she wailed.

"We'll get to that later," Dad assured her. "The important thing now is to get moved in. Spring is almost here, and we'll need all the time we can get for other things."

He would be reminded of those words many times in the years to come.

We continued our tour. The unfloored downstairs was to be the kitchen, dining room, and pantry, all in one large room. The living room upstairs was snug in size, bare of furniture, and scant of windows. An open stairway slanted down to the base-ment, and a two-by-four handrail enclosed two sides of the open stairwell. A trapdoor seven or eight feet long was fastened open by a leather strap hooked to the wall above the stairwell.

10

"What's that for?" we asked.

"To save heat," Dad informed us, pointing to the big round woodstove crouching bandylegged near the north wall. "We don't want the heat going down the stairwell when we are all upstairs in the evenings."

Off the living room on the south side were two rather small rooms. The one on the river side became my parents' bedroom. The other was destined to become Mom's sewing and general work room.

"Where do we sleep?" Danny asked.

Danny was then nine, sturdy and self-assured, the eldest son. I was seven, slender and introspective, the dreamer of the family. Bobby, the youngest, was five, towheaded, chubby and inquisitive.

"You have the finest room in the house," Dad told us.

He opened a door on the river side and we all moved out onto a large covered porch that extended the length of the house and was completely open to the world and to the elements on three sides. This room appeared to be suspended in midair but was actually cantilevered by the floor joists so that it thrust out seven or eight feet from the house and about the same distance above the ground. The hillside sloped away below us, dotted with a few oaks and an occasional clump of hazelnut brush. Between the foot of the hill and the river lay a broad, flat meadow fringed with willows. An enormous fir tree, nearly six feet in diameter, stood almost within hand's reach of the porch on the south end of the house. A railing ran around the three open sides, offering somewhat limited security.

"Now this I like," Mom said warmly.

Mom was then and remains to this day a health faddist and fresh air fiend. In the twenties some rigorous physical culturist — perhaps it was Bernar MacFadden — foisted upon the American public the conviction that abundant fresh air was essential to healthful sleep. The faithful adherents of this philosophy, including our mother, were certain that the slightest restriction of "natural" ventilation would not only be unhealthy but could produce asphyxiation. Consequently, the sleeping porch became a national fad. The three of us had slept in one of these wind chambers in our Medford home, but it at least had offered partial protection.

Seeing the skepticism on our faces, Dad said briskly, "You'll get used to it."

And get used to it we did.

chapter three
They came before us

THE FIRST WHITE MEN to visit the Rogue River were Jesuit priests who arrived in the early nineteenth century and named the area Valley of the Rogues. Their intent is still disputed by scholars. Some say the plural form "rogues" suggests that they were impressed by the inhospitality of the local Indians, a conclusion that is well supported by the ferocity of the Rogue River Wars of the 1850s. Others think that the obstreperousness of the stream coursing through the valley inspired the name, an argument that

13

also carries much merit. When gold was discovered in the valley in the early 1850s, the territorial legislature bestowed the name Gold River on the stream, but this was never adopted and after a year or so "Rogue River" became the popular, official, and lasting designation.

The earliest homes in the region were in and around Jacksonville, where gold was discovered in 1852. Within a decade or two, people were pushing farther into the hills and mountains of the Upper Rogue, attracted by its untamed beauty and boundless resources of land, water, and timber.

By 1867, Bill Rumley, for whom the source of our water supply was named, had taken up a homestead on what came to be known as the McAndrews place, the property owned by the Train brothers in the time of our residence in the area. That same year, a man named Peyton chose a tract of land at the upper end of the bench and was shortly joined by his mother and stepfather, the Sullivans, and by Samuel Taylor. These three families — Peytons, Sullivans, and Taylors — emigrated from Kansas, traveling by train to Medford and then by wagon over what surely must have been the roughest forty miles of road in Oregon. Jim Peyton, son of the original settler, was farming the family homestead at the time of our arrival, and his children became our classmates at the Laurelhurst school.

In 1886, Jeremiah Franklin Ditsworth, a saddle and harness maker, homesteaded the virgin wilderness just south of the Peyton place and raised a family of four sons and seven daughters, all of the latter being at one time or another schoolteachers in Jackson County. Like many of the other settlers of the upper Rogue country, the Ditsworths left the lower valley to escape the ravages of malaria, at that time believed to result from drinking impure water. This malady raged unchecked until nearly 1900, by which time most of the mosquito-infested ponds and sloughs had been drained to make way for pastures and orchards.

Gradually, the Ditsworths cleared away the dense forests to create one of the finest farms on the Upper Rogue, exposing rich deposits of organic forest compost to a depth of more than twenty feet. They hit upon the idea of using goats to browse down the brush and young trees, thus reducing the cost and labor of clearing land. These creatures reverted to the ways of

14

their wild ancestors in seeking the highest mountain crags. No fence could contain them when they felt the urge to climb. This habit sometimes cost them their lives, for in heavy snow the goats were doomed unless kept under cover. The snow matted in their long, coarse hair, weighting them down and freezing them cruelly to the drifts, where they became easy prey for the cougars and coyotes.

At about the same time — the late 1880s — Joe Phipps took up land two miles south of the Ditsworth claim, stayed to settle up, and in 1908 moved to Alaska, where he scratched out a respectable stake in gold. About the time Phipps filed on his homestead, a trapper named Jack Goodloe built a log cabin on the site that later became our home. After trapping out the area, Goodloe moved on and was replaced by another squatter named Gus Hammer, who stayed until his whiskey gave out, then moved back to the Applegate country whence he had come.

Around 1900, Jeff Brophy established the first formal homestead claim and "proved up" our old place. Some time thereafter Charley Toney, from whom Dad acquired the property, bought Brophy out and "broke his pick" looking for gold under the big oak trees. Other early settlers were the Vaughans, Gordons, and Taggarts, all of whom arrived before 1900.

Mail service was not instituted in the community until 1890. Prior to that, anyone "going out" for trade or other purposes collected his neighbors' mail, both outgoing and incoming. Since the rude wagon roads were generally impassable from late October through March, only three or four such trips were made on foot during the late fall and winter months. Eagle Point, twenty-five miles away by the old stagecoach road — the ruts of which were still plainly visible in our time — was the trading post for the district and could be reached in a day's journey. The outbound wagon might haul beans, potatoes, and skins of animals for the market, while staple foods like rice, flour, bacon, and coffee — together with drygoods, tools, and, of course, the mail — made up the incoming load.

Clothing was rough and made to last. The Ditsworth boys wore buckskins. "Good enough clothes when it was dry and cold," said Frank, "but not very well ventilated in hot weather and mighty heavy and slick when they got wet." The girls wore gingham dresses and sunbonnets. When store shoes wore out,

15

children and adults alike wore homemade moccasins of deer hide.

Like most pioneers, the early settlers lost no time increasing the size of their families. A school soon became imperative. In 1891 the men of the neighborhood hastily erected a small log schoolhouse, ten by ten, on a parcel of the old Phipps homestead near Lost Creek. As was customary in backwoods communities, school was held only about three months of the year, from approximately June through August when weather permitted the children to travel the rutted roads and before the farming season had advanced to the point of requiring their services for harvesting.

For a firsthand account of this early school, I share with the reader a letter from a homesick young woman who had the misfortune to be the first teacher of the little log school.

Leeds, Oregon
June 8, 1891

Miss Ida Perry
Woodville, Oregon

My dear girl:

I am at last at my destination after the hardest journey I ever took. If I had come on horseback I would not have been more sore and bruised. You know I told you I was a day behind hand. Well, when I arrived at Eagle Point Mr. Ditsworth had gone on and I had to stay all night so did not get here till yesterday. I was so tired and it was so rainy that I decided to rest today and teach Saturday. I jolted around in the wagon so yesterday that the skin is all off of the "place where I set."

It cost me just $5.00 to get to this horrid place. O I am the most disheartened girl you ever saw. Imagine yourself away up in a thick forest, in the highest hills of Or., where you hear panthers screaming all around, nothing but rocks and brush, few neighbors in log huts, a school house of logs 10 ft square (the school house is 10 ft square not the logs) and just high enough to stand in, no blackboards or anything but boards stuck up in the cracks for seats, and about a doz. children who never went to school in their life and worst of all only $20 per mo. and costs $10 every visit I make home. No place of amusement, no young folks and too far away for Tom ever to come. No wonder I am discouraged. They made me draw up the contract and I only drew it up for 10 weeks so if I can get another school by that time I will not stay here after what I have seen. I dread tomorrow. Ida, I can tell you now where I am. I am away up between Louse Creek and the source of Rogue River. Well I have done nothing but complain and I suppose you are tired of it but I can't help it. We don't get mail here only just as the neighbors needs something and goes out and takes the mail sack with them sometimes once in 3 or 4 weeks so you must always have a letter ready for me for I will nearly die for mail. O how can I hear from Tom. Ida, don't you pity me? I have no news to tell you but if I don't get a chance to send this off soon I will tell you how school goes. Write me a long letter as soon as you get this.

Mira

Mira Bedford survived her initial shock and stayed on for two years. A succession of other young teachers followed. As the community grew, so did the schoolhouse: Two more log structures were erected on or near the original site. By the time Frances Aiken (later Mrs. Pearson, my teacher at Prospect High School) took her turn in 1903, enrollment had grown to about thirty. Conditions were still primitive, with random-sized desks and benches donated by parents, much borrowing of the few available textbooks, and inadequate heat in the rude structure. Frances, suffering from toothache and chronic sniffles, wrote her father in Prospect that nothing would induce her to accept another contract.

But progress, though slow, was beginning to penetrate the frontier community. The school board installed standard desks and seats, and parents purchased textbooks. Mrs. Peyton wrote the young schoolma'am, declaring, "My children now have books, and I want them to neither borrow nor lend." The prospect of such luxurious conditions overcame Miss Aiken's resistance; back she came for another term.

In 1911 Frank Ditsworth donated an acre of land to the school district two miles up the road from the old log school. The two-room frame school we later attended was built that same year near a grove of handsome, red-barked laurels. In 1914, teacher Hattie Rose proposed the name Laurelhurst for the school, and this suggestion was accepted by the board. The district by now was fairly seething with progress: The steelgirdered, plank-decked bridge vaulted the narrow river channel at McLeod, and the road had been blasted out of the cliffs above the river to penetrate the five-mile benchland east of the Rogue, recrossing the river below the Peyton ranch. Captivated by the name, the residents started calling the road Laurelhurst Loop, and the district shortly acquired the name Laurelhurst also.

Before 1900, occasional small hunting parties from the Upper Rogue River Indian tribe penetrated the district. They were treated well by the settlers and, accordingly, were never a source of trouble. Like many other western tribes, the Rogue Rivers were horsemen when the whites first came into the country, having captured and tamed the wild mustangs that were descended from mounts escaped from the Spanish conquistadores three centuries earlier.

Not all of the wild horses fell into the hands of the Indians. One band of fifty or sixty roamed the mountains of our district when the pioneers arrived, and a remnant of these survived during our later years. Around the turn of the century, an outlaw white stallion led this herd and committed a number of depredations against the early settlers. So persuasive were his charms that many a plow mare joined forces with the wild ones. Those who resisted were mutilated and sometimes killed by the hooves of the bandit chieftain. At length a rifle bullet cut short his career of destruction. Then the terrible late winter storm of February 1917 locked the hills in deep snow for days, bringing death by starvation to all but seventeen mares from the wild band. Some of these were with foal, so the herd struggled on until the early 1950s, when the last of them were rounded up and slaughtered for chicken feed.

chapter four
School days

ONCE WE HAD MOVED to Laurelhurst, our parents enrolled us in
the elementary school, and with a mixture of dread and curiosity, we approached our introduction to this new world. Determined that we should make a proper initial impression, Mom
dressed us, that first Monday morning, in new sailor suits she
had made from a design in a ladies' fashion magazine. The navy
blouses were set off with shoulderwide square collars and long
flowing scarfs reminiscent of Little Lord Fauntleroy. The trouser

19

legs were cut short, and long ribbed stockings left our knees exposed. We wore black patent leather sandals with straps, and our hair was combed forward in straight-edged bangs. Thus attired, we fidgeted for what seemed an eternity by the mail box before the school bus arrived.

A smallish yellow vehicle with the words Laurelhurst School appearing above its narrow, vertical windshield rounded the bend and drew up before us. We climbed aboard feeling ill at ease and self-conscious, yet filled with excited curiosity. We met a barrage of silent but eloquent stares. Had the possibility of escape not been sealed by the slam of the bus door, I believe we would have withdrawn.

Four or five tousel-haired, dirty-faced boys in threadbare bib overalls and an equal number of girls in cotton dresses and cloth coats inspected us with open-mouthed astonishment. For a time their silence only intensified the strain; then the snickering began. A hoarse whisper from the back of the bus introduced us to a term we would soon come to hate: "City dudes!" Before that long day ended we had to fight several times for honor and self-respect. At home that evening, we served notice on Mom that we would never again wear the sailor suits, and we never did.

Aside from the tension of this encounter, we found the five-mile bus ride fascinating. Throughout the years, I never tired of watching the fields, woods, and streams along the narrow, winding road as the bus proceeded at a sedate pace to our destination. After we eventually divested ourselves of the "city dude" image and gained acceptance among our companions, we joined in the general chatter that always enlivened this ride. A month or so after our enrollment, the entire trip was devoted to the exploits of a lone aviator who was reported to have flown the Atlantic in a single-engine airplane.

The place appointed for our instruction proved to be a two-room white building of conventional rural American schoolhouse design, belfry and all. About twenty-five children attended the lower eight grades, all in one room. Six or eight older ones constituted the high school student body in the adjoining room. An elderly, gray-haired teacher named Mrs. Edmunson presided over the elementary pupils, who ranged from cherubic first-graders to muscular louts of sixteen or so. The eldest was Lester Naught, whose attendance was spasmodic and whose assessment of school was summed up in a statement our father was to quote for the remainder of his life: "Cain't learn nawthin' there!"

There is something to be said for Lester's opinion. Considering the rude conditions, the range of ages of students, the variety of demands on the teacher, and the crowded classroom, one may wonder how anyone ever obtained any education at all in the American one-room schoolrooms of a generation or two ago. The truth is that there were in fact some advantages to this arrangement.

As the day progressed, each class would rotate to the front of the room for an hour's instruction while the others, presumably, studied for their own classes. There was, of course, a temptation to mischief and time-wasting inherent in this system, but there was also an opportunity for the studious ones to review classes they had already completed or anticipate others still ahead.

Mrs. Edmunson was nervous and irritable and seemed unequal to the scope of her responsibilities. When the spitballs began to fly she would glare around wildly and rap the head of every boy within reach of her ruler. For some reason she took a particular dislike to me and once remarked that I was "too stupid to know beans with the bag open." This precipitated a confrontation with Mom that was resolved only by Mrs. Edmonson's retirement at the end of the school year.

Once I took a prized Christmas present, a new pair of boxing gloves, to school to try out on my peers, who still needed to be convinced from time to time that city dudes were not necessarily sissies. Mrs. Edmunson insisted on being my first opponent. This idea utterly appalled me, not through fear of defeat or physical damage but because of the dreadful spectacle I would create in fighting an old lady in front of the entire school. But she was not to be denied, and presently, like one in a trance, I found myself squaring off on the very schoolhouse steps with a most unlikely opponent — a gray-haired apparition with skinny arms festooned in purple boxing gloves, which she flailed inexpertly in my direction. Her shrill, cackling laughter was as unnerving as her appearance, and I made certain not to land a punch. The bout ended inconclusively.

After the first year Mrs. Edmunson was replaced by Mrs. Nye, whom we all liked immediately. She was tall, blonde, cheerful, and athletic, and we considered ourselves lucky when we were chosen on her side for basketball games during recess or lunch hour. After a couple of years she moved away and was succeeded by Miss Fitzgerald, who was dark, soft-spoken, and alluringly shy. Once when the school bus was returning late from a county track meet I shared a seat with Miss Fitzgerald. The older boys and girls were pairing up and trying to act romantic, which bothered me, as I was at the time miserably shy around girls. I seemed to sense in Miss Fitzgerald a kindred spirit as we sat in the darkened bus, made sparse conversation, and tried to pretend that the giggles and hoarse breathing around us were perfectly normal sounds.

The school grounds were situated on the pie-shaped, one-acre wedge of land donated in 1911 by Frank Ditsworth. The school building, a covered playshed, a woodshed, and two privies were located at the wide side of the triangle. The play area sloped gently and inconveniently down into the point of the wedge, adjacent to the road. Above and to the east ranged the densely timbered Rogue River Mountains.

The proximity and position of these mountains determined to a surprising degree our extracurricular activities, for the school buildings and grounds lay in deep shade on winter mornings until perhaps ten o'clock. Clear skies and freezing nights prevailed through much of the winter, so the bare red clay earth tended to freeze into a crunchy, unstable, crystalline top layer two or three inches thick until mid-morning. Then it melted into a red soup until the late afternoon sun partially dried it out. Before the drying process was complete, the sun was gone and freezing began again.

This daily cycle resulted in perpetually muddy floors and continuing complaints to the school board by the teachers. At length the board members laid a few long planks in the muddier areas, primarily between the schoolhouse and the girls' privy, presumably in the belief that the boys' shoes would inevitably get muddy anyway. To our delight, these boards became covered with heavy frost which, with a bit of sliding, turned into a coating of ice. The big thrill for the boys at recess was to slide on these planks, challenging propriety by coasting to a stop as near as possible to the entrance of this forbidden facility without actually violating its sacrosanct inner premises.

Our other playground activities included Annie-over-the-woodshed, workup baseball, dirt court basketball, crack the whip, tag, and improvised gymnastics on the rings, swings, and bars in the playshed. Once Bobby Peyton was struck in the mouth by one of the lead-weighted rings; his upper lip remained permanently thickened by the injury.

During lunch period we sometimes explored the wooded area near the school grounds, where we climbed the limber dogwoods until they bent to the ground. Then we slid off and allowed the trees to snap back into their normal position. After each of these bendings, the wood fiber lost some of its resiliency until eventually the young trees were permanently bent into lovely arches, recording for future generations their contributions to the joys of our childhood.

In the fall we gathered the huge sugar pine cones, each as large as a loaf of bread, and carried them back to the school yard to be used as ammunition. To this day I can remember the surprising impact of a blow in the back of the head from a well-aimed sugar pine cone.

Winter snows brought a different war game. Snowball fights raged until all combatants longed to quit but dared not, and only the school bell mercifully terminated hostilities. With hands half frozen, we crowded the red-hot woodstove, the heat from which sent shafts of pain through our fingers that made the cold from the snow a pleasure by comparison. Only then would we heed the teacher's advice and thaw our hands gradually under the cold water tap.

The mothers of the neighborhood took turns sending a large kettle of soup for hot lunch. This savory broth was heated on the big stove, and the aroma from the pot became maddeningly distracting as the noon hour approached.

Dear, bygone Laurelhurst school days: How I would love to relive them.

chapter five
Squirrel ranching

SPRING CAME EARLY that first year. In only a few weeks we were becoming accustomed to the rawness of our new life and finding joy in it despite many hardships. There was no running water in the house, and rural electrification was still ten years away from the Laurelhurst district. As the snow melted along the path to the outdoor privy and the sun warmed its unpainted sides, even that chilly forced march began to seem less an ordeal than an adventure. We began to linger a while, marveling at the treasures displayed in the Montgomery Ward catalog.

With the mild weather came sudden, heavy rain, lasting for many days and rapidly thawing the snow in the mountains. Nearby, every dry ravine turned into a torrent. One morning about three weeks after we came to our new home we awoke to an astounding sight. From our balcony bedroom, we looked down, not on the familiar willow-girded meadow but on the Rogue River itself in swollen, raging flood. On its muddy crest it bore huge stumps, clumps of brush, great uprooted trees, and every conceivable form of flotsam. As we stared, a manmade structure bobbed past, turning slowly on the swirling current.

"Look, Daddy!" I cried, pointing. "A house! Maybe there's somebody in it!"

Dad shook his head. "No, it's only an outbuilding. Somebody's henhouse, I'd guess. But that river could carry a house if one was in the way. It reminds me of my dad's stories of the Johnstown flood back in '89."

Mom was staring intently at the place where the river flat had been just yesterday. She turned and gave Dad a look we couldn't fathom.

"Perfect place for a fish hatchery, isn't it?" she asked wanly.

Dad shook his head glumly and said nothing.

We were not the first — or the last — of those living on the river to discover that the Rogue had been aptly named. Since the early publicity by Zane Grey, and later by Edison Marshall and other popular writers, the Rogue had become a legend that attracted many, especially Californians, to build their homes along its banks. So great was the appeal of the famous stream that people often insisted on building as close as possible to the water. Like the tourists at Crater Lake National Park who annually courted disaster by trying, despite warning signs everywhere, to pet the deceptively friendly-looking bears along the roadside, these new settlers ignored both the name and the reputation of the mighty Rogue. We were glad that Dad had built our house high on a hillside.

The flood subsided in a day or so, leaving shallow ponds everywhere on the river flat and tangled driftwood lodged in trees and willow bushes. Surprisingly little serious damage was evident in our community, but downstream, we learned, it was another story. Pastures and orchards had been turned into useless gravel bars, cottages had been torn from their foundations, and bridges had washed away. At Savage Rapids Dam, west of Medford, the footbridge over the river had been swept away, and this loss has never been replaced. Thus the flood of 1927, as though commemorating our arrival, took its place in local history as one of a half dozen great Rogue River floods dating back to 1851.

During the period of those floods, the Rogue River Valley had undergone exploitation of its timber resources that rivaled the sacking of Carthage by the Vandals. Timber crews had slashed brush, bulldozed and dynamited roads, diverted streams, and burned huge mounds of waste as they attacked the seemingly limitless stands of fir, sugar pine, and cedar covering the steep slopes of the Rogue. Very early they discovered the superior efficiency of clear-cutting, and thereafter, wherever their hobnailed boots trod, desolation followed. Clear-cutting worked greater damage on the dry interior valleys, such as those of southern Oregon, than on the moist coastal forests where reforestation took place more readily.

But the loggers were never able to enlist the Rogue in its own destruction, for so swift and rapid was the current that the rafting of logs was impossible. In the early days, logs were hauled out of the woods by ox teams, later by trucks. Towering pyramids of virgin logs thundered down the Crater Lake Highway, forcing passenger cars off the road, as the truckers sped for the valley sawmills. At the mills each load added to the mountains of logs dominating the flat landscape. Lumber was king in southwestern Oregon, even to the point where its very predominance threatened its own health as well as that of other industries. Younger lumbermen saw private operation as the shortest route to financial independence and overcrowded the field. In numbers greater than the region could support, they quit the mills and shouldered heavy mortgages for trucks and equipment, gambling on success where many had failed before them. This excessive pressure drove up the price of stumpage and hastened the desolation of both the natural environment and the economy.

But even the Rogue could not indefinitely withstand the heavy assault by the loggers, for their operations left the river banks torn and scarred and vulnerable to erosion. In the winters of 1889, 1890, 1910, and now again in 1927, the river had fought back in its own savage fashion, and the devastation wrought in those historic floods was awesome. We wondered, as we watched from the safety of our hillside home, what future rampages we might witness, and what the effects might be on our lives and fortunes.

As the warm spring days brought forth new growth to cover the flood ravages, we turned our attention to the unfamiliar new life that confronted us. Even the most routine activities associated with everyday living presented unexpected problems, and for each of these our resourceful father found an ingenious solution. Most of his solutions, however, involved a good deal of work.

Dad made use of two springs that oozed from the grass within a hundred yards of the house, although their combined flow was insufficient for all our needs. The nearer spring was unsuitable as a water supply but it served well as a cooler after Dad built a low structure over it to protect the food, which remained surprisingly fresh and sweet for several days in this improvised refrigerator. The other spring, situated higher on the hill, was clear and pure and provided excellent drinking water. Dad dug it out to a depth of five feet or so and formed a reservoir by placing two concrete culvert pipes in vertical position, one above the other. A conical steel cover fit closely and kept out insects, frogs, and garter snakes. Six inches of gravel in the bottom filtered the incoming water, and a pipe in the side released a trickling overflow into a grassy pool.

The spring provided water for cooking and drinking but was insufficient for bathing, laundry, and house-cleaning. For these requirements, we used a rainwater cistern in the winter months, then switched to carrying water, first from nearby Bobby Creek (named for my younger brother) and later, when this tiny stream dried up, from the river. I was designated bearer of water from the spring, but all three of us were needed to carry water from the creek or river.

This latter task was laborious and sometimes unproductive as boisterous spirits and sibling rivalry overcame our devotion to duty. Two tubs and two buckets were involved in the process as we formed a chain with Danny between the two tubs and Bobby and me flanking him, each with a tub handle in one hand and a bucket swinging from the other. When uneven ground caused one of us to stumble, the other two usually got a shoeful of water, and this precipitated a good deal of unnecessary staggering, jostling, and sloshing. When we arrived at the house with our trousers soaked from the knees down and the vessels less than half full, Mom always made us go back for another load. This water was stored in a forty-gallon wooden barrel just outside the kitchen door.

Fuel was free, abundant, and close at hand. Dad loaded the new Montgomery Ward dragsaw into the wagon and hauled it to a fallen tree. We positioned the saw against the log — usually a sizable fir perhaps three feet in diameter — and stabilized it by hammering the iron "dogs" into the wood with a sledgehammer. Then we waited while the gasoline engine drove the long blade in even strokes. As each round fell, one of us rolled it aside and split it into pie-shaped sections with sledge and wedges while the others repositioned the saw and repeated the process. The horses loafed in their traces until the wagon was loaded; then we headed for the woodshed.

Most of the heavier work — hauling, plowing, dragging, and the like — was horse-drawn. Our two geldings, Jerry and Barney, had been purchased from Frank Ditsworth. Barney, a phlegmatic old gray, did what was asked of him and never gave us any trouble. Jerry, a potbellied bay, did not look particularly aristocratic but considered himself above hard work. Although strong enough in build, he disliked labor and had a positive genius for faking effort. Unless the driver was on the alert, his performances were convincing, as he knew how to keep the traces taut without extending himself in the slightest. He also objected to being ridden and had perfected a technique for discouraging this practice. Whenever he felt a saddle on his back he inflated his belly while the girth was being cinched, then expelled the air as the rider climbed aboard so that we usually wound up on our own backs instead of on his. When this failed, he attempted to scrape us off by plunging under the low-hanging barn roof. Anyone who thinks a horse is a dumb animal should have known old Jerry.

Dad's dream of raising fish commercially was doomed to a short life. He pursued the subject with the hatcheryman at Rogue

Elk, five miles downstream, where the submerged wiers collected spawning Chinook salmon by the thousands. The man stared at Dad incredulously.

"You must have a lot of money, mister," he said bluntly. "If you can afford to start a fish hatchery, you don't *need* to start a fish hatchery."

It was, of course, only a dream; the realities necessary for its fulfillment had never touched Dad until that moment. He had no capital, no connections, no knowledge of a market — nothing but an unsupported desire to earn a living by raising fish. As he stared around him at the complex system of buildings, machinery, and instruments, the dream burst like the bubbles surfacing in a nearby tank.

With characteristic stoicism, Dad concealed his disappointment and turned his thoughts and talents to the meager opportunities that our new circumstances offered. In those times, just before the Great Depression sent the nation's economy reeling, employment was available with the crews that maintained the Crater Lake Highway, and Dad hired on with one of these. After the crash, when President Roosevelt formed the Civilian Conservation Corps to work on public lands and parks, Dad obtained a job as a tool repairman at Crater Lake National Park. For a time he drove the district school bus, and during the 1930 census he helped count noses in the backwoods of southern Oregon. As times got worse and jobs scarce, it was commonly believed that only Democrats could get government work, so Dad swallowed his Republican pride and registered as a Democrat in order to stay in the running for the dwindling number of available jobs.

Although we did without many of the things we had taken for granted in Medford, one thing we did not lack was space. The tract of land for which Dad had paid old Charley Toney three thousand dollars consisted of 205 acres stretching a full mile along the southeast bank of the Rogue River. At times our minds boggled at the thought of such wealth. At other times, because of its unsuitability for agricultural or other commercial exploitation, Dad referred wryly to the place as our "squirrel ranch." Although much of it was covered in small pines and oak, with here and there a majestic fir or sugar pine, the prevailing growth consisted of brush — manzanita, chaparral, and, on the river flat, willow. Nowhere was there a stand of quality timber in a quantity sufficient to warrant commercial cutting.

Each year, Mom planted a garden in the tract in front of the house. Diligently, she enriched the thin soil with scrapings from the chicken coop and a vile broth of cow manure and water that she kept standing in a wooden barrel at the garden's edge. She ladled out this foul-smelling potion to encourage a lagging cornstalk or a wilting potato plant as necessary. Weeding fell to Danny and me, Bobby being too small to handle a hoe in the early years. I came to detest this chore, although it was certainly preferable to cleaning the chicken coop.

As our first spring turned into summer, we reveled in the daily sunshine. It soon became apparent, however, that our first garden would not survive the intervals between the brief and infrequent rains. "How are we going to water this place?" Mom demanded.

Dad, the Purdue man, was always more of an engineer than a farmer, so this question caught him unprepared. As usual, he turned to the highest available level of technology for his solution.

There was, he discovered, an old dry ditch skirting the hill north of the house. He learned that it led to a wooden flume across a fairly wide ravine about a mile up the road. A short distance beyond the flume, the ditch connected to Rumley Creek, a year-round stream of fair size. Furthermore, miracle of miracles, our property title included water rights to this precious source!

Although the flume was battered into uselessness by many years of falling trees, and the ditch was a veritable sieve of digger squirrel holes, the real problem lay at the lower end, nearest the garden. Here the ditch rounded a shoulder of the hill above our house and abruptly disappeared into a shaly incline of greenish rock, fifty feet higher than the garden level and — what irony! — no more than two hundred yards from the languishing vegetables. Between lay a small ravine — Bobby Creek — and a pasture adjacent to the old log barn.

Dad pondered the problem and came up with one of the most ingenious of his many desperate solutions. A reservoir at the terminus of the ditch clearly was essential, but how to make it? Excavation was out of the question because of the bare, sloping rock. A tank moored to the hillside seemed to be the answer, but it would have to be a very large tank, and that meant a large amount of money. Then he remembered from his Medford welding shop days an old steam boiler that had become obsolete and was destined for scrap. Negotiations commenced, and presently Dad brought home an enormous rusty cylinder, five feet in diameter and perhaps twelve or fourteen feet long. We stared at it curiously. An inspection port in the top — or side, who could tell? — was barely large enough for access. The inside was full of pipes, perhaps fifty, running the length of the boiler, each welded securely at either end of the tank.

"How will you get water from this thing to the garden?" Mom asked.

"By pipe," Dad responded.

"And where will you get the pipe?"

Dad drew on his old briar, and the familiar twinkle came into his eye. "You'll see," he said.

And then began the incredible undertaking of removing fifty welded pipes from the inside of the boiler. Dad brought out his torches and tanks, climbed into that rusty old boiler, and started cutting pipe. Smoke curled from the entry port, blue light flickered, then there was a clang, and shortly another pipe slid through the end of the boiler. Two days went by, and we heard the final clang. Dad climbed out stiffly, raised his hood, wiped his begrimed countenance, and surveyed an impressive stack of rusty pipe. The next day he began welding the joints of pipe together in a ribbon of steel that slanted down the hill, jumped the ravine, crossed the pasture, and eventually arrived at the center of the garden.

We were profoundly impressed, but our elation was subdued by the thought of the remaining obstacles.

"How will the tank hold water with all those holes in it? And the flume? And the ditch?" we demanded.

Dad produced a sackful of tapered cedar plugs, turned on a lathe by a friend of his, and proceeded to drive them into the holes from the inside, fitting each plug into place and relying on the water to swell and hold it when the tank was filled. He positioned the old boiler on two concrete cradles and welded the pipeline to the tank.

Repairing the flume was simple carpentry involving a thousand or so board feet of rough lumber from a neighbor's sawmill. Danny and I began alternating weekly at "walking the ditch," shovel on shoulder, patrolling from flume to tank. We plugged squirrel holes, shoveled out limbs and leaves, and patched the bank where it had been punctured by the hooves of cattle and deer.

For me, this job offered many rewards. The river roared below, casting its primeval spell over my spirit. Deer occasionally broke from cover, and often the flume would yield an eight- or nine-inch trout, escaped from Rumley Creek and stranded in shallow water.

Near the end of my tour, I would turn aside and stand for a few minutes on the rim of a rocky cliff, out-thrust from the steep hillside, and survey the surrounding woods for wildlife. Some-times a rabbit would hop away, or an owl — disturbed by my sound and baffled by the daylight — would swoop soundlessly from his perch and disappear in the deep forest. Finally, with great reluctance, I would break the spell and finish my tour of duty, rounding the shoulder of the hill within a hundred yards of my cliff and emerging at the tank.

Dad was so pleased with his irrigation system that he added a couple of refinements for good measure. Where the ditch arrived at the tank he devised an automatic overflow shutoff. This con-sisted of a cedar float in the tank attached by a pulley-and-wire linkage to a gate in the ditch. When the tank was full, the pulley wire went slack and the gate fell of its own weight, closing the inlet and letting the surplus water flow into Bobby Creek instead of crudely spilling over the top of the tank and down the rocky hillside. This was technically impressive, but the other feature was far more functional. Taking advantage of the splendid fall from ditch to garden, Dad installed an elevated sprinkler system that covered the entire garden, thus eliminating the labor of ditching and flooding. It was a grand moment when we stood watching the leisurely sweep of water pelting the parched gar-den, which by then was nearing the crisis point. Mom's eyes beamed with joy.

"I should have known you could do it, Norm," she said.

This technological triumph carried our family a long way toward social acceptance. Then, even more than today, and especially in remote and thinly populated rural areas, residence did not automatically constitute belonging. For a year or so, the farmers tended to stand apart and regard the newcomers as city slickers. But when our neighbors witnessed the deliverance of the dying garden, they nodded their heads in approval.

The twenty or thirty old apple trees that came with our property were diseased but still somewhat productive when we arrived. We cherished the firm red fruit, even though fully half the crop was of poor quality. Dad found an old cider press, and in the fall we chopped up the culls to make gallons of sweet cider, which we traded to the Groceteria in Medford for staples.

We were not the only ones who appreciated the apple orchard, it seemed. Woodpeckers drilled the rough trunks for beetles and sometimes sampled the fruit as well. At night, porcupines prowled in search of tender bark, wreaking havoc on the scant new growth that the overage trees produced. Hearing the dogs cry the alert, Dad would reach for flashlight and rifle. We boys, of course, went along and later took over this duty. On one occasion, Danny pumped at least twenty rounds of .22 bullets into a prickly marauder at point blank range before the poor beast tumbled from the tree. The next morning we had the considerably less exciting job of burying the carcass before the dogs started muzzling it.

Our dogs, it seemed, harbored an implacable antagonism toward porcupines and never learned to leave them alone. Time and again, the Chesapeakes would come whimpering home from the woods, muzzles white with quills. Dad would mutter an exasperated oath and go out to the shop for his pliers. He always needed one or two of us boys to hold the patient still while he yanked out the barbed needles, bringing a yelp with each extraction. Sometimes the quills were imbedded so deeply that they had to be drawn through the dog's flews from the inside. These operations often required a full half hour, even after we became accomplished at our bloody work, and Dad would finish by washing off the crimson muzzle and slapping the tormented victim, half in sympathy and half in disgust. Often enough, the same dog would be back for the same treatment within a week.

Another resource — this one of modest but significant commercial value — was the abundant supply of small fir trees scattered over the hills. These we cut for Christmas trees and sold on consignment through a Medford service station. The market price ranged from fifteen to fifty cents, depending on size and symmetry, though an unusually fine specimen might bring as much as seventy-five cents. No one would pay a dollar for the best Christmas tree in Oregon in those days. With luck we could add a few dollars to our small Christmas earnings by sending along some mistletoe.

"Turkeys ought to do well here," Dad speculated one day, looking for still another source of income. Mom responded with interest, and another venture was born. (Dad, the imaginative innovator, conceived most of our money-making schemes and Mom usually got the job of implementing them.)

It was fascinating to watch the turkeys adapt to the rolling hills and flatlands, seeking isolated natural nesting areas and scorning the luxurious accommodations Dad offered them. Mom soon realized that the silly birds could not cope with their wild environment unaided, so she appointed herself their guardian. First she had to locate the nests. Ranging across the countryside, she quickly learned their habits. The hens favored places offering the best concealment for eggs and young birds — ravines, thickets, and wooded areas. She learned also that turkeys, though well equipped with camouflage, cannot conceal the round and glittering eye, the one feature that is incompatible with a natural setting.

Gradually a meandering path developed that took Mom to every nest, and she marked each with a small strip of white cloth tied to a nearby bush. At an appointed time in her busy day she made her rounds, counting eggs, noting any new hatches, and wiping beaks. Young turkeys, she discovered, have a distressing susceptibility to respiratory infections. Dad referred to this daily errand as "Mom's turkey trot."

Aside from the occasional depredations of coyotes, the turkeys did well, as Dad had forecast. Their strange behavior patterns afforded a good part of our daily entertainment. As the young matured and the flock grew in size, they banded together and went wherever they chose, there being no fences high enough to restrain their wanderings. They tended to focus their activities on two large level areas, one below and one above the house. We called these places "flats" because no other term seemed to properly describe them; they were too desolate to be called fields or meadows, the lower being thinly covered in

34

sparse, dry weeds and the upper in chaparral and manzanita brush.

At any rate, these two areas offered some attraction to the turkeys, who would amble slowly up the hill, foraging for grass-hoppers along the way. After an hour or so, the upper flat would lose its appeal and the entire flock would take flight and soar downhill over the house, gobbling noisily in midair, and settle on the river flat. After sampling its meager fare for a time, they would edge toward the hillside and repeat the performance. They usually managed about three of these spectacular flights a day.

Hawks and coyotes normally were a threat only to the smaller birds. Once all achieved flight status the flock was fairly safe. When any of the young were attacked, the older birds defended them courageously, so our losses were surprisingly small con-sidering the extent to which the turkeys were allowed to fend for themselves. An unexpected benefit was the efficient alarm sys-tem invariably provided by the entire flock in the presence of a rattlesnake. They would all form a tight circle around the snake, with every neck stretched toward the rattler and every wattle aquiver, all gobbling like maniacs. We soon came to recognize the dependability of these warnings and got in the habit of taking a hoe or shovel along when investigating such noisy signals. Always we would find, coiled and vibrating its nerve-tingling message of death, one of the huge rattlers that infested the area.

We had many encounters with rattlesnakes, and the fact that none of us was ever bitten must be attributed more to divine protection and the sluggishness of the snakes than to any pru-dence on our part. Twice I narrowly missed placing my bare foot on a coiled rattler.

On one of these occasions, while stepping over the hewn log threshold of our old barn, I responded to some providential nudge and looked down to see the flat, triangular head and familiar patterned loops directly in my path.

The other time I was hunting with my single-shot .22 rifle on the upper flat and again felt warned to look where I was about to place my foot. Both experiences produced spasms of horror, but neither these nor any of the other incidents caused any of us to develop a lasting fear of snakes. Mom, who soon lost her city ways and seemed to us the most intrepid of frontier-women, once slew a gigantic reptile with ten rattles and a button only a few feet from her kitchen door.

My parents often lingered at the table after meals, discussing ways of bringing in some money. As our original savings dwindled and the Depression began to settle upon us, these conferences took on increasing urgency. Mom and Dad had the notion that the rugged splendor of the local setting, plus our unrefined style of living, somehow constituted potentially commercial resources. Often as they wrestled with these ideas, I heard the term "dude ranch" mentioned. Several difficulties stood in their way, however.

First, they lacked the expertise, and particularly the showmanship, for this type of venture. Second, as with the fish hatchery scheme, they were hopelessly undercapitalized to provide the buildings, horses, and trappings essential for a western resort. And finally, fewer people were able to take expensive vacations of this type. So this idea, too, came to nothing.

They did, however, attempt a minor variation on the dude ranch theme. Acting on a conviction that our place would make a fine boys' summer camp, Dad composed a flowery advertisement, full of blandishments and half-truths, and ran it in the classified section of the Medford *Mail Tribune*. We waited impatiently for results. The ad ran out, but nothing happened.

"Maybe you should have made it a little stronger," Mom worried.

"It's probably already too late in the season," Dad said. But he ran another ad, even more artful than the first, and this time there was a response. A Medford widower visited, inspected, and finally agreed to lodge his two sons with us for a month. A modest fee was agreed upon.

My mother was barely able to suppress her excitement. She was certain this was the beginning of a thriving enterprise — profitable, pleasant, and socially beneficial to her own sons as well as to the lodgers.

The boys arrived and their father departed after getting them settled. We eyed them suspiciously, and they returned our stares in kind. By now we had lost not only the look but also the outlook of city dwellers, and these urban visitors in their neat clothes seemed to us offensively civilized. We could not have been any more prepossessing in their eyes. A pair of faded and ragged bib overalls constituted our only summer garment. Our bare feet were calloused, grimed, and tough as the paws of a bear cub. Our hair was tangled and unacquainted with a comb except during infrequent barberings by Mom, who used the famous bowl technique.

No thought had been given to organized activities, the idea apparently being that our clients would enjoy themselves more and gain a richer experience by being left alone than by being regimented. Nevertheless, we three boys were expected to act as guides and companions, a responsibility we accepted only grudgingly.

We were at the time boarding a pair of saddle mares for a Central Point rancher. We had also acquired a pair of woolly black chaps, which we shared, and inexpensive wool felt sombreros, which increased in value in our estimation as they deteriorated in shape and cleanliness. Thus equipped, we considered ourselves dashing cowboys and spent endless hours galloping across the river flat and pestering our yearling heifer with our homemade lassos.

Our guests, the Barrett boys, naturally insisted on sharing in this activity, and we reluctantly gave them each turns in the saddle. Unfortunately, Mollie, the buckskin mare, had developed the habit of veering sharply to the right whenever she saw a path leading in that direction. We had become accustomed to this aberration and had learned to counter it by reining her to the left when we saw temptation looming, but we failed to impress this problem upon our guests. Within a week, Kenneth Barrett went flying from the saddle and broke his leg.

The rest of the boys' camp experiment was anticlimactic. Feeling uneasy in these hazardous and rustic surroundings — not to mention the limitation imposed on Kenny by a knee-length plaster cast — the two city boys spent most of the balance of their stay hanging about the yard reading funny papers (as comics were then called). We returned to our familiar activities — playing cowboy, swimming, exploring islands in the river, and, under protest, performing our chores.

Everyone was relieved when the month was over. Nothing was said about renewing the classified ad.

chapter six
Neighbors

ONE DAY EARLY in our first summer a small man with an incredibly large mustache appeared at our door, carrying a soiled cloth bag. We eyed him suspiciously, thinking him to be an itinerant peddler, but he smiled disarmingly and identified himself as Jan van der Maas, our nearest neighbor. We had seen his name on the mail box near the cliffs but had seen no house nearby. He explained that he lived some distance from the road and invited us to come visit him. From the dirty bag he produced some enormous carrots. It was our first and only housewarming gift. Mom was deeply touched.

Soon after this visit we were informed by other neighbors that Van, as the old Dutchman was called, lived alone without so much as a cat for company. They were at pains to tell us also that he was a poor housekeeper and was considered eccentric though harmless. Most of the people of the community avoided him, which seemed not to bother him in the least. Mom was intrigued by the idea of having a hermit for a neighbor and was inclined to accept the gentle old man at face value. She invited him to call again, which, from time to time, he did. Soon a preposterous rumor circulated in the neighborhood linking Van and our mother romantically. This silly gossip, more than any other incident in my recollection, epitomized the meanness, suspicion, and bigotry of many country folk, especially in hard times.

In truth, Mr. van der Maas was one of the openest and purest spirits I have ever known, unique in that his life gave faithful witness to his simple, unselfish philosophy. His deep religious faith seemed to have come partly from his Dutch Reform upbringing and partly from his adult experiences, which he gradually pieced together for us.

He was born in Holland, but very early in his childhood his parents had moved to South Africa, where he grew up. After completing his education, he became a schoolteacher, but his career was soon interrupted by the outbreak of the Boer War. All the young men were immediately conscripted. A small but gallant band of farmers, the Boers — who were trained from earliest childhood to shoot game at extreme ranges across the broad savannahs — inflicted heavy losses on the British. Their own casualties, however, together with the sufferings imposed by the two-year war, brought the Boers to their knees. Britain showed compassion, initiating peace overtures to prevent the stubborn Afrikaners from committing mass suicide by continuing the struggle in the face of certain defeat. A small pension for his war service now sustained all of Jan van der Maas's simple needs.

Like many of the young veterans of his country, Van left South Africa after the war. He came to the United States, took out citizenship papers, worked for a few years on the Milwaukee Railroad, then came west. How he found his way into the hills of

Jackson County and located in his curious hermitage was never explained, at least to my understanding.

Although our relationship with this free spirit was never as sympathetic as Mom's, we boys used to like to visit Mr. van der Maas. For me, at least, one reason lay in the enchantment of the forest path leading to his shack. The trail rose steeply from the river road to a stile — that quaint and seldom seen structure best known from Mother Goose — over a woven wire fence. It then coursed through a deep wood, over a hill, and along a gentle, winding ravine for nearly half a mile.

There was a fairy-tale quality about this short walk, perhaps instilled by the unfamiliar stile, the pristine wood, and the odd little man who could often be heard singing as we emerged from the trees into the clearing where his house lay, a barren place where thin pockets of soil covered a rocky outcropping. His selection of this desolate site in preference to the charming glade from which we had just emerged could only be explained by a cluster of small springs that watered the pinch of soil on which his garden was located. An eight-foot fence surrounded the garden to keep out deer. A weather-beaten unpainted shack, a small privy, and a flimsy-looking woodshed flanked the bare yard.

Van routinely greeted us without surprise, although he might not have seen another human in a month. Usually we brought along some gift, which he accepted with satisfaction. Once Mom sent him a pullet, partly to keep him company and partly to augment his meager food supply. Five months later we learned that he had kept every one of the eggs provided by his little companion, and he turned them over daily in a box of sand "to keep dem fresh." As he showed visitors through his garden he warned them not to step on his pets. These turned out to be a pair of rattlesnakes he kept to control pests. Of all his wild neighbors, only the digger squirrels and the grasshoppers bothered him.

"Dey come from de whole vorld in," he complained.

His garden, which provided nearly all of his diet, consisted mainly of root vegetables, which he preferred because of their bulk and because they were less susceptible to grasshopper damage than leafy vegetables. Van ignored the niceties observed by most gardeners, who harvest the vegetables while they are still tender and succulent. He allowed his turnips and rutabagas to grow until they were coarse and strong and full-sized. We boys regarded with distaste these eccentric practices and generally shared our neighbors' scorn for the old hermit's peculiarities.

When his shoe soles wore out, Van patched them with hacked-out pieces of tire tread. His garden was fertilized with horse droppings that he painstakingly collected from the nearby hills: "following the ponies," Dad called this tidy custom. Frank Pettigrew, a young neighbor who did most of Van's outside provisioning, disclosed that the annual cost of these supplies amounted to as little as thirteen dollars.

Van's cabin was littered with old papers and magazines, mostly religious tracts and metaphysical publications from many lands. Mom asked him why he didn't buy a radio for entertainment. Mr. van der Maas was astonished at the suggestion. "Vy?" he asked. "I entertain mineself!"

And so he did. As the years passed he sang and read and meditated and worked as necessary to sustain his modest needs. Clearly, he was the most contented spirit in the community. Once he volunteered to sing an Easter solo at the Sunday worship service, then being conducted at the McLeod store. The neighbors were somewhat taken aback at this offer but, at the appointed hour, they were even more amazed when Van appeared, more presentably attired than ordinarily, and sang "The Holy City" all the way through in a fine tenor voice.

COMPANIONS OUR OWN AGE were few and distant during our years on the Rogue; so few, in fact, that an attempt to organize a Boy Scout troop failed because of a shortage of eligible candidates. But about a mile and a half from our place, near where Big Butte Creek flows into the Rogue, the Elmer Glass ranch on the old Crowfoot Road formed the nucleus of what social life the community afforded its youth. "Buck" Glass had two daughters — Erma, who could hit a baseball as far as any boy, and Lois, whose early adolescent femininity made us aware that girls were not exactly the same as boys. Their cousins, the three Rogers boys of about our own ages, lived in a rustic cabin at the edge of

Butte Creek. Leo Hoag and Jack Casey were teenagers four or five years my senior and about the same age as Erma Glass. The Harding girls, Dorothy and Maxine, and Tommy Close were ex-Californians recently arrived in the community.

High on the hillside above the Glass ranch in a weather-beaten shack nearly a mile from the nearest road lived Jim and Robert Thomas, two brothers only a couple of years older than we were. When we first came to the Laurelhurst district, their elderly parents also lived in the little shanty, but age and poverty had since driven them out. Their grown children in the lower valley near Medford were now caring for them and would have made provision for the two younger boys as well, but Jim and Robert refused to go, preferring the uncertainties of their hillside home to a stifling city life.

Robert's chest was caved in from an early, untreated case of rickets and his hair was perpetually dusty and uncombed. He seemed quite dependent on his older brother Jim, who was husky and good-looking and remarkably self-reliant, though an indifferent scholar. With game swarming in the hills above their shack, the two brothers never lacked for food as long as there was ammunition for the battered .30-30 carbine. Jim could shoot a rifle from the hip and drop two deer together almost before they could spring from their beds.

Whenever the opportunity offered, I tramped the hills with Jim, marveling at his woodsmanship and enjoying his undemanding company. Late in the afternoon, we were apt to wind up at the pasture down at the Glass place, where the two girls, their cousins the Rogers boys, and perhaps my own brothers and one or two others might be found playing work-up baseball.

Sometimes we lingered at the house or returned after supper to sing songs while Erma played the piano. Other groups may have sounded better on such favorites as "Ramona," "K-K-Katy," and "When the Moon Comes Over the Mountain," but none ever rendered them with more fervent sentiment. While we harmonized under the unshaded light bulb (the Butte Creek district was well ahead of us in getting electricity), the taciturn rancher reclined wearily in wool socks, long underwear, and overalls, and his apple-cheeked wife smiled to herself, knitted, and rocked.

Much of our free time was spent in the vicinity of the Big Butte Creek bridge. A hundred yards upstream the creek (which is really a small river) tumbled over a six-foot fall, where we stood by the hour in late summer to watch the salmon leap. Time after time, the big Chinook would shoot up from the foaming pool, only to slip back and have to try again. Always they eventually attained enough height to propel their straining, quivering bodies into the upper cataract, and once there, they struggled fiercely against the current until they reached slack water. Under the bridge, the spawned-out sorebacks offered easy targets for rocks or bullets, and though we knew the seriousness of such offenses, we sometimes gave in to the urge. One day, absorbed in this sport, we failed to notice another presence until a long shadow fell across our feet. We looked up into the frowning face of Ed Walker, the long-suffering district game warden.

"You boys had better leave those fish alone," he said grimly, "or you're going to get your tails in a crack."

On another occasion my brother Danny, Kenny Rogers, and Jim Thomas were exploring the woods near this bridge when they came face to face with a half-grown skunk. Characteristically, Jim seized the initiative. Remembering that skunks can only attack while standing still, Jim lunged forward and the other two followed. In an instant the skunk was leading them in a wild chase over hummocks and logs and around trees and bushes. The little animal darted and dodged while the three pursuers panted, yelled, lost their footing on the slippery pine needles, and wondered how they had gotten themselves into such a predicament. Still they charged on, since there seemed no safe way to cut short the chase without risking a counterattack.

Meanwhile, my younger brother Bobby and Cecil Rogers were out on the bridge throwing rocks at a mud turtle perched on a log downstream. As the racket of the chase drew nearer, they found themselves directly in the path of an onrushing skunk followed by three frantic, exhausted boys. The skunk, seeing no other way to escape these converging human forces, launched himself into space and landed in the stream below, where he swam to safety among the overhanging willows and disappeared. Buck Glass watched all this from his adjacent pasture with no evidence of amusement or surprise.

43

"Next time," he said dryly, "you might ketch him. Then *you'll* be the one that wind up in the crick."

CASEY'S CAMPGROUND — now called Casey State Park — lay along a deep, swift reach of the Rogue where trout and salmon swarmed and huge cottonwoods cast their dappled shade. Like their competitors, the Hoags, who lived half a mile to the north, the Caseys were geographically outside of the Laurelhurst district by virtue of being across the river, but both the Caseys and the Hoags were closely knit within the fabric of the community.

The Caseys offered rustic cottages at reasonable rates, and many Californians vacationed there each summer. Mrs. Casey ran a small restaurant and store, while Jim Casey kept up the cabins and picnic grounds and performed as a sort of theatrical manager to the premier attraction of the enterprise: Jerry the bear.

Jerry padded back and forth on a heavy chain that slid along a cable. His range of movement was delineated by a long, low enclosure of fir logs laid end to end and elevated a foot or so above the ground. He was of impressive size, black and glossy, and held an irresistible fascination for the passing tourists. His favorite act was to stand on his hind legs and swill bottle after bottle of a rich chocolate beverage that the tourists bought for him in order to get him to stand still for picture taking.

To my knowledge, Jerry's exact capacity for chocolate pop was never established, although his record for a single day was about a hundred bottles, which he dispatched one Fourth of July. The Caseys always kept an ample supply of this beverage on hand and gauged their total business by Jerry's consumption. Thanks to their furry shill, they prospered throughout the long years of the Depression.

Directly across the river from us but a mile distant by road and bridge, Elmer Hoag operated the McLeod grocery store, gas station, restaurant, and campground. One of our great summer delights, when we had a nickel to spend, was to walk to the store for candy or soft drinks. The restaurant was a seasonal business, catering chiefly to the tourists, as dining out was an impossible luxury for the local populace. Mrs. Hoag specialized in chicken dinners and homemade pies. Her daughter, Evelyn Coburn, waited on the diners, who were seated at rustic tables varnished to a glittering patina. From the adjoining store, we peeped enviously through the glass door at the prosperous-looking patrons.

OUR NEAREST NEIGHBORS to the north were the Train brothers, Orin and Marion, who operated a ramshackle sawmill. Orin, who had never learned to read or write, could scale a stack of lumber to the inch and never make a mistake. Their houses were typical frame farmhouses of that period, surrounded by old cars and broken-down trucks. The setting for these humble dwellings, however, was worthy of a baronial estate. Their properties lay in a broad meadow of stately oaks and rich fields, watered by Rumley Creek and nestled against the mountains. The Trains supplemented the uncertain earnings of the sawmill by farming a portion of their acreage and poaching on a scale that made the rest of us seem positively law-abiding.

One year after I had returned to Medford, I learned that one of the boys, who was about my own age, had been caught by game wardens with the still-unskinned bodies of eleven does and fawns in the rumble seat of a Model A Ford. Such wanton slaughter being inexcusable even in those times, he was wintering in the Jackson County jail in Medford. When I went to visit him, pondering how I might cheer him up, I found him in the best of spirits. The food was good, he said, and the accommodations exceeded in luxury anything he had ever experienced. "They even have sheets on the bed!" he marveled.

In a mountain district barely emerging from frontier status, the flourishing, modern Weeks pear orchard — four miles up the Laurelhurst road from us — was a startling sight. The property had been homesteaded in 1892 by W.F. Taggart, who had bought out Joe Phipps's squatter's rights. A decade or so earlier, a man named Joseph H. Stewart had moved into the lower Rogue valley and pioneered commercial apple and pear growing in southern Oregon.

In 1898, Mr. Stewart and a son-in-law, Dillon Hill, were fishing on the upper Rogue. The orchardist immediately appreciated the possibilities of the Taggart property, which had deep, rich soil and an abundant water supply. More important from the standpoint of pear production, the remoteness of the

45

setting offered immunity from the diseases already spreading among the lower valley orchards. Before the sun set, Mr. Stewart had bought the Taggart place, and soon he and another son-in-law, Arthur J. Weeks, were setting out their mountain orchard.

The results confirmed Joseph Stewart's vision: soon the benchland was yielding astonishing harvests of fine, cull-free pears. Other interests in California called Mr. Stewart away, and he deeded the property to A.J. Weeks, who bought additional land and continued to develop the place with assistance from his young son, Stewart Weeks, named after his grandfather. In 1920, Arthur Weeks inherited a business in Berkeley that required his presence there, and he formally deeded the property to his son.

By the time we arrived in the Laurelhurst district, Arthur Weeks had returned to the log cabin built by his father-in-law in 1899 to spend his last days on earth. Shortly after his death, his widow also passed away. Young Stewart Weeks remained on the old place and continued the enterprise begun by his grandfather.

A soft-spoken gentleman in his mid-thirties at the time we arrived, Stew Weeks held the respect of all his neighbors, but his quiet reserve discouraged close friendship or familiarity. He served on the school board and donated freely of his time and substance to community activities. In late summer, when the pear harvest came on, he provided employment for thirty or forty local people.

Although we were rapidly shedding the last of our urban veneer, we found the ways of some of our neighbors shockingly primitive. Not infrequently, girls married at thirteen or fourteen and were toothless grandmothers at thirty. From the road we sometimes saw babies and toddlers running naked through the woods. The boys picked their noses, seldom wore underwear, and urinated on their hands for warmth while waiting for the school bus. Moonshining was so commonplace that it has been estimated that some five hundred stills may have operated at various times and places between Medford and Prospect during the thirties.

Despite these crudities, the people, by and large, were decent, reasonably generous with their scant possessions, and respectful of other people's property. No one in the community ever thought of locking a door.

---

chapter seven
The rugged life

DAD QUOTED Edgar Guest's poem, — "It takes a heap o' livin' in a house to make it home," — whenever any of us expressed dissatisfaction with our frontier life style, which Mom especially did, in fairly forthright terms, during our early days on the Rogue. But the softness of town living soon hardened into sinew.

The sleeping porch, that spartan development of the times brought to its ultimate rigor by Dad's conception of Swiss architecture, initiated the toughening process. Danny and I occupied a double bed near the door, and Bobby had a single bed to himself at the north end of the long, elevated veranda. Not recognizing how much warmth our dual arrangement was generating, Danny and I couldn't understand why poor Bobby complained so bitterly of the cold. It seemed to us that he was nesting under a mountain of blankets, yet he cried nightly for more covers. Our own bed was like a snug cave, thanks to a heavy canvas tarpaulin drawn over the entire bed, including our heads. Often we would shake an inch of snow from the old tarp as we scampered indoors to escape the sting of the winter wind.

Inside, the house was not much warmer. The banked embers of the potbellied heater upstairs had long since died, and the kitchen below was as cold as a dungeon. The daily task of lighting the cookstove was a function we learned to accomplish with minimum delay. With the temperature sometimes hovering near zero, our fumbling fingers sought out the pitchiest kindling and applied plenty of crumpled paper to the tinder. Warmth came with surprising speed.

Some people claim that a wood-burning cookstove imparts not only a special warmth to the kitchen but also an exceptional flavor to food. Whether this is true, I cannot say; but those who have never warmed themselves before an old-fashioned kitchen stove have yet to learn the real meaning of the word "cozy."

After briskly disposing of her morning calisthenics on the sleeping porch, Mom took charge of the kitchen and soon had it steaming with delicious smells. Frequently, breakfast was cornmeal mush or oatmeal porridge. Sometimes it was johnny cake with thick syrup and crisp fried potatoes. Usually there was some kind of fruit, such as rhubarb or applesauce or, in early summer, fresh strawberries.

Early on, we had acquired two temperamental Jersey cows, whom Dad, with his flair for grandiose titles, named Cinderella and Sarsaparilla — Cindy and Sassy for short. Morning and evening, each of these high-strung bossies permitted us to relieve her of a quart or two of very rich milk. One of our great luxuries was to drown our cereal or strawberries in thick, sweet cream, which Dad called "clotted Devonshire." We didn't worry about cholesterol in those days, having never heard the word.

After breakfast, the three of us hiked up to the road to wait for the school bus while our parents plunged into an endless round of toil. Dad busied himself in the workshop or the barn, and Mom attacked her household duties — washing, mending, cooking, preserving, and preparing for her daily turkey trot. At the end of the school day there was plenty of work waiting for us, too. Mom pointed to a pair of galvanized two-gallon buckets, and I headed for the spring. If the weather was fine, she usually had to call me back about twenty minutes later.

Then there was wood to be chopped and stacked behind the kitchen stove and in the upstairs woodbin. Mom, who normally permitted us to work things out our own way, was meticulous about the size, variety, and amount of wood that was to be stored behind her cookstove: so much pine, so much oak, and so much fir, each in a variety of sizes; some pitchy and some resin-free.

At the time, I could neither satisfy nor comprehend such rigid standards and was in constant trouble for failing to provide the specified assortment. Later I realized that cooking on a woodstove, like playing a musical instrument, is more art than science and demands continuous subtle adjustment. Attaining and holding the desired temperature became a personal contest between my mother and the stove — a battle, as she conceived it, against a stubborn and treacherous enemy. So grimly involved in this struggle did she become that in another place, when she had an electric range at her disposal, she still insisted on treating it as a fiendish adversary. When Dad tried to explain all the knobs and dials to her, she told him shortly, "Never mind. Just let me battle this out myself."

Danny and I took turns milking Cindy and Sassy, an arrangement that may have accounted for their extreme nervousness, since milk cows do their best for one familiar, gentle pair of hands. In our ignorance we made matters worse by tying their legs to limit their prancing about, as we grew tired of being stepped on or left stranded at the milk stool. Even when tied, however, they continued to slash us with their manure-encrusted tails, so we took to binding legs and tail together rigidly, a practice frowned on by all experienced dairymen. They responded by giving even less milk than before.

Sometimes the two Jerseys got tired of it all and, finding a convenient hole in the rail fence, went AWOL. Worst of all, they didn't find it necessary to come home at milking times as milk cows normally do, for their stingy udders never became so distended as to give them any discomfort. We had to hunt them down and drag them home at rope's end, a tedious and time-consuming job, for their ways were unknowable and, even when captured, they resisted being either led or driven.

Another, more sinister cow incident occurred about 1930. It was common practice in those days for cattlemen of the lower valley to drive their animals up into the mountains in early spring to let them range on Forest Service land, then round them up in the fall for either market or local wintering. However, as times grew worse and the beef market declined, the cost of baled hay became an increasing burden to the ranchers. Some marginal operators took to leaving nonmarketable cows in the mountains through the winter to forage for themselves on moss and chaparral in the hope that they might fend off the prowling coyotes and survive until the demand for beef improved.

Close as we were to the high range, these strays were a great nuisance to us, as starvation frequently drove them to knock down our rickety rail fence wherever they might glimpse a tuft of grass on our side. Once on our property, they would trample the ditch bank, muddy the spring, or cause some other disturbance. Dad issued standing orders for us to round up any such strays and drive them off the place, then to locate and mend the hole in the fence through which they had entered.

One day late in March, Danny and I came upon a mean-looking stray at the foot of the hill not far from the house. When we attempted to get around to the other side and drive her toward the gate, she swung her gnarled head perversely and plunged between us, galloping clumsily toward the river. Off we went in pursuit, hoping to flank her where the stream cut short her escape. But she plowed straight into the icy current and waded to the island where, in summer, we swam and experimented with Bull Durham cigarettes. We followed, slipping on the round rocks and snagging our clothes and hands on blackberry thorns.

At the upper end of the island the river current was wider, swifter, and deeper; it was here we felt certain of bringing the outlaw to bay. But she eluded us again and, half swimming, half wading, made her way back to the mainland. Shivering, floundering, and hurling threats, we pursued the gaunt beast. She climbed the low bank and abruptly came to a stop. We approached warily, expecting another maneuver, but we needn't have worried. The poor, starved creature's energies were finally exhausted. She faced us, spread-legged and motionless except for the heaving of her bony ribs. In a spasm of exasperated fury, Danny picked up a round river rock, perhaps twice the size of a chicken's egg, and flung it. It struck the cow's forehead with a thud, and, to our horror, she collapsed on the river bank and expired with a groan.

After the initial shock, our first thought was that any value the inferior meat might have would soon be lost unless properly bled, so we hacked the cow's throat with our pocket knives. As blood gushed out on the rocks, we took a closer look and, to our further dismay, recognized the brand on the angular hip. Our hearts sank in despair.

Near Eagle Point, the Mayhew family had lived on their ranch since the 1860s, each generation exceeding its predecessor in notoriety. (Indeed, this is the only family whose anonymity I feel compelled to preserve; hence, the "Mayhews" bear pseudonyms.) At that very moment, Ron Mayhew was serving a prison sentence for killing a man in a drunken brawl. Toughest and meanest of all the Mayhews was old Red, Ron's father and current ruler of the clan. The brand on the dead cow was clearly that of Red Mayhew.

"What do we do now?" moaned my brother.

"Make it look accidental," I said. With considerable difficulty, we managed to break a lower foreleg over a large rock. Then we rolled the carcass down the bank, partly to make it less conspicuous and partly to explain the cause of the broken leg by the position of the body. In our terrified haste, we disregarded the obvious inconsistencies in this series of actions.

At home, Dad listened to our story in silence, puffing impassively on his pipe. At last he said, "Well, you guys did it. The consequences are on you."

We howled our protest at this parental abandonment, but Dad remained unmoved. Mom said nothing.

Two weeks went by, and the incident began to fade from memory. Perhaps, we hoped, our crime would go undiscovered and the scavengers would dispose of the evidence. Then one day, quite unexpectedly, a slouching figure on horseback appeared at our big ranch gate. The faded mackinaw and battered black sombrero were unmistakable. It was Red Mayhew! Danny and I bolted for the house. Dad looked very serious as he walked to the gate. The hunched rider waited, reeking menace, so it seemed.

With our eyes barely above the window ledge, scarcely daring to breathe, Danny and I watched the ensuing tableau. The rider didn't dismount, and Dad didn't offer to open the gate. Ten minutes went by. Fifteen. Then, Mayhew abruptly lifted the reins, flicked his horse, and wheeled off up the driveway.

"What did he say?" we demanded when Dad returned to the house.

He gave us a look that wasn't especially friendly. "What do you think he said?" he snapped. "He said, 'Can you explain what happened to one of my cows that I found down by the river with its leg broke, its throat cut, and its head bashed in?'"

Knowing our father to be a truthful man, we dreaded his reply as we asked, "What did you tell him?"

Dad answered evenly, "I told him I didn't know a damn thing about it. Furthermore, I told him if he would keep his stock on his own land, nothing would happen to them."

And to our vast relief, we heard no more about the matter.

TO ME, IT SEEMED evenings were the most pleasant times of all. Work done and supper over (we quickly fell into the country way of calling the evening meal supper), we would troop upstairs, Dad leading the way with the big white-gasoline lamp. I brought up the rear with a bucket of drinking water. The trapdoor was lowered, closing off not only the cold breath of the earthen-floored kitchen but also, symbolically, the workaday world. The bucket sat on the railing that enclosed the stairwell. Hooked to its rim was a large granite cup. For the next two hours or so we lost ourselves in peace and quiet contentment.

Dad placed the lamp in the center of the table, pumped it to capacity, tamped his pipe with Granger Rough Cut, and settled with a vast sigh in his big leather chair, the latest issue of the *Country Gentleman* or the *Saturday Evening Post* in his lap. Mom sometimes mended, but sometimes she too read. Her usual reading matter was a religious tract or Bernar McFadden's *Phys-*

ical Culture Magazine or a pamphlet of practical instruction from the County Extension Office.

In fact, until we got our Crosley battery-powered radio, we all read. My favorites at that time were *American Boy Magazine*, with its interminable installment thrillers by Clarence Buddington Kelland, and books by a writer named Altsheller about the Fearless Five, an intrepid group of Indian fighters of singular purity and resourcefulness. We read with deep concentration and enjoyment, interrupting ourselves only to fuel the fire, pump the lamp when its white glare subsided, or visit the water bucket. Sometimes Mom produced a dish of sliced apples or some hazelnuts in the handpainted wooden nut bowl.

It was about 1030 or 1031 when Dad brought home the Crosley radio, and with it, a total change in the tempo and style of our evenings. Now the supper table was cleared with dispatch, the dishes given a lick and a promise, and the procession up the stairs accomplished at quickstep. There were then only a few radio stations, and only two or three of the strongest transmitters reached us through the surrounding mountains, so there was little arguing about program selection.

Amos and Andy, those universal favorites, came on first. On different nights Fred Allen, Jack Benny, Fibber McGee and Molly, and the Gilmore Circus kept us enthralled. The Shadow and the Lone Ranger maintained justice without remuneration. H.J. Kaltenborn and Walter Winchell described the frenzied activities of a world so fascinating, yet so remote from our own, that it seemed unreal. We learned about Babe Ruth and Red Grange and Bobby Jones. In 1928 Herbert Hoover had easily disposed of Al Smith, "that Tammany Hall papist," Dad called him. Now the good gray president faced a stronger threat by another New Yorker, the urbane patrician, Franklin Roosevelt. On Sunday afternoons, Father Barber dispensed homilies and managed somehow to keep One Man's Family safe within his smothering, patriarchal dominion.

Then one evening at a crucial turn in the drama, the magic voices faded into silence. We stared, first at the radio, then at each other, then at Dad.

"The battery's dead," he told us. "What now?" we wanted to know, expecting him to restore the sound immediately.

"Next time I go to town I'll have it charged," he said.

This was a totally unacceptable response, but the times and our father being what they were, we had to live with it. Then, to our delight, we learned that the battery retained a latent flicker of life, permitting it to recover a little of its power each day, enough perhaps to keep the set going forty minutes the first evening, thirty-five the next, and so on. Like shipwrecks rationing precious rainwater, we metered the dwindling reserves to the last whisper. Then it was back to the books and magazines, for no amount of wheedling would induce Dad to take the thirty-two-mile trip to Medford a day earlier than was demanded by the normal requirements of marketing and provisioning.

At the time we left Medford we were a two-car family, a rarity in those days. The old Dodge delivery truck was actually a smallish van, a slab-sided black box, homely but functional. The cab was upholstered in black leather, and the extras included a manually controllable spotlight and a klaxon horn that emitted a harsh *Oooo-Gaaaah!* preposterously out of character with Dad's sedate driving habits.

The other automobile was a Stevens touring car, very nobby in its day, with long, low lines and a tombstone-shaped grill. A tool box was bolted to the running board and a unique compressor, operated by engine pressure, permitted inflation of tires independent of service stations. Our reduced circumstances did not permit the luxury of two cars, so Dad jacked the Stevens up on blocks in the barn, thus preserving the tires, and covered its rakish lines with a tarpaulin to protect the beautiful fabric top from being fouled by the swarms of bats nesting high among the logs. There it remained from 1927 until 1932. Meanwhile, we seldom drove anywhere except as necessity dictated.

Accordingly, our rare visits to Medford were as precious as they were infrequent. During the school year such trips were scheduled for Saturdays so the whole family could go. Dad loaded the truck with such marketables as the season might provide — apples, cider, and dressed turkeys in the fall; Christmas trees and mistletoe in early winter; and later, after he and Mom had mastered the necessary surgical skills, fat capons of surpassing quality. Mom climbed in beside Dad, and we piled into the van or, in fine weather, rode the tailgate. This latter position was not as hazardous as might be thought, for Dad believed that thirty-five miles an hour was fast enough for all but the most catastrophic emergencies. Such a leisurely pace gave us ample time to take in the passing scenery, or as much as could be seen from the back of a truck.

Medford by now seemed to us a veritable metropolis. Dad always called it "the wicked city." Its population of fifteen thousand gave it an atmosphere of size, activity, and significance not found in the hamlets of Shady Cove, Trail, and Prospect. The stately homes of East Main and South Oakdale looked like mansions and even our old place on South Holly, with its quasi-mission architecture, seemed elegant. Mom always became a little subdued when we passed that way, so Dad soon found reasons to avoid our old neighborhood.

Commerce was always the first order of events. Dad went straight to the old Gates & Lydiard Groceteria, forerunner of the supermarket. There he dickered with Mr. Lydiard, whom I cannot recall ever seeing without his set, managerial smile. Our produce brought us a few dollars in trade, never enough to cover our purchases. Clerks in long aprons loaded great burlap and cotton bags of staples — flour, sugar, rice, and cornmeal. Almost everything was in bulk. The oil from the peanut butter always soaked through the carton on the long trip home, requiring the addition of vegetable oil to restore its spreadability.

After trading, Dad looked in on his old cronies along Front Street while Mom purchased the minimum of clothing and dry goods necessary to get us by until the next trip, perhaps three months away. If time and cash permitted, we young ones slipped off to the old Rialto or the Roxy for that rarest of all treats, an afternoon movie. Tom Mix and Douglas Fairbanks were popular heroes, but if Hoot Gibson or George O'Brien happened to be playing, it was a major event for me. Armed only with manly virtue and courage, Hoot was impervious to all the dangers of Western outlawry, and George O'Brien's immense biceps and granite smile were charisma personified. I waited breathlessly for the inevitable chase, when good old George invariably rode under a big oak tree and grabbed a low-hanging branch, executing a giant swing and landing behind the saddle of his pursuer, whom he then dispatched with ease.

Then there was always a trip to the library, where I checked out another Altsheller thriller and pored over the shelves until my parents came to round us all up for the homeward trip. The last stop was at the edge of town, where Dad dropped in on some friends who regularly saved the comics from the *San Francisco Examiner* for us boys. On arriving home I always took the entire pile straight to the attic and sorted the daily and Sunday issues separately in exact chronological order to ensure proper continuity of the serials. Popeye always seemed to be getting lost in burning deserts, where he crawled endlessly on hands and knees toward waterholes that always turned out to be mirages, while vultures perching in the giant cacti leered at him obscenely. Barney Google was a dapper urbanite who occasionally visited a backwoods ruffian named Snuffy Smith, who was later to supplant the star.

Sometimes an editorial page appeared in the pile of comics. The Hearst political cartoons of the day were grim in contrast with Krazy Kat and the Captain and the Kids. The Bolshevik Revolution was a major concern of that era. Gruesome scenes depicting heaps of corpses and countless starving children haunted my dreams, and in one chilling cartoon the Four Horsemen of the Apocalypse galloped through oceans of hollow-eyed, spectral humans. I shuddered at these hideous images and returned to the world of Maggie and Jiggs.

To us as boys, the daily problem of outwitting starvation became more a lark than a hardship. Resources not normally available came readily to hand, and otherwise proscribed practices were excused because of the hard times. Poaching, for example, lost most of its stigma and risk but somehow retained its excitement. Throughout the Depression, the game wardens simply looked the other way. Deer were plentiful in the hills, and trout and salmon swarmed in the river.

Our formula for obtaining venison was almost monotonously simple, as deer tend to feed in the same familiar haunts each night. Such a place existed conveniently close to the road and less than half a mile from our house. Where the benchland above us swung northward into a clump of pines, a small herd used to gather nightly at about nine or ten o'clock. Approaching this place in the Dodge, Dad would switch off the lights as he turned in from the road through pine needles imprinted faintly from our previous forays. Slowly, he swung the big swivel-mounted spotlight secured to the windshield post. Soon yellow eyes gleamed from the trees. At night, a deer's eyes are easily distinguishable by color from a cow's eyes, which appear red in the glow of an electric beam. Dad would step from the cab and make his selection without haste while we tried to still our pounding heartbeats. Then the old .30 '06 Springfield would bellow its deadly message and the night's butchering would begin.

Jack-lighting has always been the most popular method of poaching deer, because the animals usually become hypnotized by the unfamiliar light and stand perfectly still. A neighbor, whose name had best be omitted from this account, once fashioned a platform high in a fir tree overlooking a spring and planted a block of salt nearby. One night while he and his son and another man crouched on the perch waiting for sounds of deer, the nails gave way and all three plunged abruptly to the ground, thirty-five feet below. The son remembers plummeting through the air and seeing his father falling beside him, still hugging his knees in a fetal crouch. The son's fall was broken by the boughs and he slid down unharmed, but the older men sustained fractures, lacerations, and lasting humiliation.

Fish was, if anything, easier to come by than venison, for our property was at the upper end of one of the largest spawning beds in North America, extending intermittently for seven or eight miles downstream and numbering tens of thousands of fish at the peak of the season. In mid-July the mighty Chinook started appearing, still bright from the ocean, their vigor scarcely diminished and their flesh still red and firm. As summer turned to autumn, the later runs of salmon had to fight harder against the low water to reach their destination. Snouts battered and fins whitened from abrasion, these "sorebacks" struggled feebly to reach the spawning beds and carry out by instinct their life's objective, the ancient reproductive ritual. We never tired of watching the great fish, plainly visible in the deep, clear pools.

First the female would select a deposit of clean sand and gravel, sufficiently sheltered from the current to hold the eggs in place when laid. Then, rolling on her side, she would scoop a hollow nest with several thrusts of her powerful, spadelike tail. Finally, hovering over this nest, she would pump out a stream of red-gold globules. After she swam away the male would come and eject a stream of rich white sperm into the nest.

Soon after these rites were performed, the salmon would roll over on their sides and allow the current to carry their dying bodies down among the riffles, where their stench hung over the river until the November rains raised the water and flushed out the rotting corpses.

As with other species, the salmon exposed themselves through the reproductive process to many dangers, the greatest of which was the rapacity of their neighbors. During the spawning season, bear and coyotes prowled the shallows and eagles and ospreys perched in the tall firs along the river. Schools of trout darted among the beds, gorging on the eggs. We, too, joined in the plunder.

The brighter fish, when clear of bruises, were quite palatable, though not comparable in quality to ocean-fresh salmon. These we took with spears in the Indian style. Dad experimented with several styles and eventually developed a long-handled, barbed trident that worked very well. Armed with this weapon, one of us would approach the selected prey stealthily, calculate the true depth of the fish's position (a deceptive calculation because of the illusion created by light refraction), and try to pin the victim to the river bottom with one swift thrust. Only after the wild thrashing subsided was it safe to lift the big hooknosed creature out on the river bank.

Mom spurned the spear in favor of a plain pitchfork. Because this tool was barbless and relatively limited in range, her technique involved a swift, decisive, swooping motion similar to that used by bears. Still, she became quite adept and seldom came home empty-handed. One day, while surveying with satisfaction a silvery monster flopping at her feet, she chanced to look up, only to meet the impassive gaze of the local game warden, who was standing across the river. Showing no sign of surprise, he finished his inspection of the area and drove away.

The soreback salmon were foul and useless except for dog food; nevertheless, in this lowly form they constituted an important resource, for we had brought several grown dogs and perhaps half a dozen pups with us when we moved to our river home in 1927. The Chesapeakes developed a passion for this dish and also, tragically, for the raw carcasses they soon learned to scavenge from the water's edge. To our dismay, this predilection proved not only disgusting to us but also fatal to the dogs. Time and again, they would break free of all restraints and follow the carrion scent to the river bank, where they would feast and roll in the fetid carcasses, only to pay with their lives for this indulgence.

At the time, we believed the black blood along the salmon's spine to be toxic, but biologists have since learned that the Pacific salmon of northern California and southern Oregon feed upon an ocean snail that harbors flukes, which are parasitic flatworms that penetrate the liver of a dog and bring agonizing death. The call of the river eventually destroyed all of our magnificent Chesapeakes.

When the salmon runs were over we captured trout in a chicken wire trap, which we submerged in deep water and secured at the upper and lower ends by wires fastened to underwater tree roots. The downstream end was closed, the upstream end open in an inverted funnel tapering to a restricted orifice well down in the trap's maw. Trout, which head upstream and drift downstream, entered this device in dozens and were usually still swimming inside when we came by to check our catch. Once we captured nearly a hundred at one time. On another occasion, we found a huge otter drowned inside the trap, having apparently met its fate in pursuit of a captive trout. Dad sold the pelt to Ed Fleming of Jacksonville for ten dollars.

One day when the three of us had been sent to Bobby Creek for water, we discovered lurking in the tiny pool where we filled our water vessels a three-foot-long Chinook salmon. We raced up the hill to report this phenomenal encounter, only to find our parents unwilling to believe our story. Then something mysterious in Dad's manner gave us a clue. He had found the salmon in the trout trap and had gone to the trouble of moving it alive to Bobby Creek as a joke on us.

With the early spring rains there invariably appeared, among the willows on the river flat, clusters of spongy morel mushrooms which we cleansed of sand and clinging humus. Dipped in egg batter and cracker crumbs and deep-fried, these succulent fungi provided many a delicious meal. We also enjoyed various species of wild berries and nuts in season and occasionally partook of quail and other small game. When this wild fare became tiresome, we sacrificed a young rooster or an undersized turkey, usually a fowl of low market value.

One day a flock of Canada geese, storm-driven from their

normal flyway, alighted on the river flat below our house to rest and look for feed. We watched the great birds with mounting excitement. Our parents were away at the moment, so Danny, who was then about eleven, got Dad's big ten-gauge shotgun down and laid its ornate Damascus barrels over the porch rail. Taking careful aim, he pulled both triggers. The recoil sent him spinning, but he brought down a goose. This triumph was short-lived, however. Mom made us pluck the gaunt bird, which cost us a precious Saturday afternoon and gave us no satisfaction, for the sinewy flesh was tougher than venison jerky and nearly tasteless.

Another time, Dad burst in to announce the discovery of a bee tree. We threw shovel, axe, crosscut saw, tubs, and buckets into the Dodge and piled aboard. Dad drove to a place not far distant from his nocturnal poaching haunts and got out. The bee tree was a medium-sized oak with a hole in its trunk about ten or twelve feet above the ground. Only a few bees were in evidence, and these were lethargic, it being only mid-spring as I recall.

We set to work with the crosscut, apprehensively keeping one eye on the blackened hole in the tree. When the bees' activity increased, ours diminished, and vice versa. Presently the tree creaked, swayed, and toppled. As it struck the ground, it split wide open at the major fork where the hole was located. Bark, dead twigs, and wood dust flew, and a ball of honeybees exploded from the splintered trunk like birdshot. We dropped our tools and scattered for the sheltering pine woods.

After ten minutes or so, Dad built a smoky fire of oak leaves to discourage the still swarming bees, and we set to work with cup and ladle to harvest the waxy comb and dark brown honey, now spreading in thick pools in the hollow of the broken tree. An appalling quantity of trash came with the honey — twigs, bark, pine needles, and dead bees. No matter, we took it all and later strained it through cheesecloth at home. The taste was at first disappointingly wild and strong, as venison disappoints the palate accustomed to beef; but we soon got used to it and ate it all with relish. The entire harvest amounted to more than ten gallons.

When my son Steve was a little fellow, my tales of Oregon left him confused about the time frame in which these incidents from my boyhood occurred. He was sure that I must have fought

Indians in my youth. And as I think of the sharp contrast between our way of life in the thirties and that of many Americans today, those events do indeed seem to belong at least another half century earlier. All things considered, these were among the most precious days of my youth.

chapter eight

Hard times

AS THE GREAT DEPRESSION spread like a vapor across the nation,
the people of our community, as elsewhere, accommodated
themselves variously to its chilling reality. Hard work and self-
denial were commonplace, almost universal, therefore tolerable.
Overwhelming debt was another matter. Inability to obtain, by
any contrivance, what seemed the bare necessities first enraged

and ultimately discouraged even the bravest. Worst of all must have been watching the sufferings of one's own children. As boys, we didn't know, except by sensing the growing anxiety of our parents, that there was even a problem.

Gradually the state and federal governments began to offer assistance. In those days it was called "relief," not "welfare." The social connotations of that term are forever etched on my mind, for soon it divided the community into two irreconcilable groups — those who applied for assistance and those whose pride would not allow them to "go on relief." The latter group considered independence essential to self-esteem and felt that taking a "handout from Washington" was somehow immoral. Some even refused to associate with those who took help from the government. A residue of this attitude can be seen today in the relatively few older persons applying for food stamps, despite the fact that this program was largely intended to assist the elderly poor.

But as the grim years began to grind us all down, pride gave way to necessity and the ranks of dependency swelled to alarming numbers. Nevertheless, our family and many others stuck to their principles. Although my mother recalls her humiliation at being unable to accept invitations because she had nothing suitable to wear, she refuses to this day to admit that we were ever poor. And I must admit that, although our toes sometimes peeped out the front of our shoes, and there were years when our total annual income must have been less than four hundred dollars, we never went hungry.

In retrospect, I suppose that eventually Dad might have yielded and applied for aid had he seen his brood in genuine physical distress, but I believe it would have quenched his spirit forever. Today I can detach myself from the harsh, judgmental attitudes of the thirties and regard with compassion those beaten hill folk who were forced to seek help. Nevertheless, I salute my parents for somehow managing to avoid that extremity.

A few years ago, when our Seattle garbage rates went up for the third time in two years (this time adding the stipulation that garbage cans must be left at curbside), it set me thinking about our Rogue River days. The next time I saw Mom I asked her, "How did we take care of trash disposal? I know we didn't have any garbage service."

"Why, don't you remember?" she said. "The dogs and cats ate the table scraps; vegetable peelings went back into the garden; and we threw tin cans down Toney's old mine shaft out under the oak trees."

And that, I now remembered, accounted for just about everything. There was no need for the weekly removal of a hundred or so pounds of discarded plastic toys, broken electric appliances, empty wine bottles, and cast-off clothing. No one worried about running out of space for sanitary landfills or ensuring that products were biodegradable. We simply didn't throw enough stuff away to create such problems.

Leaky buckets were patched and used for a lifetime. Equipment was heavy and made to last. Implements were designed to facilitate, not frustrate, repair: Wood, iron, and leather could be used to mend articles originally made of those materials. When the roof leaked, we split sugar pine shakes or cedar shingles and fixed it. When our shoes began to open at the sides, Dad bought a black iron shoemaker's last and became a tolerable cobbler, substituting square-cut copper nails for thread. Stick-on soles were cheap and easy to apply, though atrociously ugly.

Although sewing was never one of Mom's favorite activities, she took up mending out of necessity and devoted a good part of her time, especially evenings, to darning socks, patching overalls, and stitching ripped seams. Patched clothing was such a common sight in those days that it evoked no notice and caused no embarrassment; in fact, new clothes were so novel that they made the wearer more self-conscious than did worn and mended garments.

By today's standards, personal hygiene was sketchy, medical and dental treatment almost nonexistent. Today, dentists frequently encounter in older patients recognizable signs of "Depression mouth" — grotesque defects resulting from neglected repair in childhood. In spite of it all, we were remarkably healthy and seldom knew a day's illness beyond an occasional sniffle. In summer our bathing consisted of taking a bar of soap along when we went for a swim in the river. In winter we crouched in the big galvanized tub, taking turns in the same overworked bathwater unless the cistern was full from heavy rains, in which case we could luxuriate in clean water.

On laundry days, a large copper tub, long and narrow with

rounded ends and vertical sides, was filled with water and placed on the cookstove. Our grubby socks, shirts, and overalls were boiled in a strong solution of homemade soap until the kitchen was filled with steam and the smell of lye. Then we agitated the clothes with a long-handled plunger and rubbed the coarse cloth against a corrugated glass washboard until our knuckles bled. We wrung each garment by hand and rinsed the wash in two round tubs. Overalls, being long and heavy, were hardest to wring dry, and I could never manage this job to Mom's satisfaction. Finally, weather permitting, we hung the soggy garments on the line outdoors and let the soft breezes and warm sun do the rest.

The times and events through which we lived shaped not only our activities and the outward manifestations of clothing, grooming, and housing, but our very values and attitudes as well. One is tempted, under the euphoric fallacy of the "good old days," to exaggerate the benefits of a rigorous and simple life. Indeed there were benefits, just as iron is tempered by the stresses of the forge, but those hard times also exerted destructive forces on our personalities. Perhaps it is enough to acknowledge that each of us was profoundly altered by the Great Depression without attempting to arrive at an exact balance between good and bad.

The most obvious effects were the simplifying of life and the reduction of choices. What one couldn't afford, he learned to do without, presumably starting with the most frivolous and proceeding grudgingly toward the most basic. It would be a mistake, however, to assume that it always worked out so, or that it does now. People, being people, sometimes turn the thing around. Since we violently resist all forces that threaten our individual selves, it is often the very thing that seems most trivial and expendable in our lives, from an outsider's point of view, that we are least willing to sacrifice. Therefore, under pressure to retrench, we gradually cast off what seem to others the most vital necessities while clinging desperately to some cherished frippery.

In the thirties, a harsh, barren decade when philistine values generally prevailed, this very human tendency was sometimes misunderstood and therefore was subject to censure. It seems to me that those who made such judgments were ignorant of — or insensitive to — the deep resolve within the human spirit that motivates all of us to protect our personal treasures as a child protects a rag doll. Proof of this may be seen in the fact that the cosmetic industry flourished throughout the Depression, and clothing styles were as gaudy as in the best of times. At twelve, I prized my bellbottom blue jeans with red inserts at the flaring cuffs. The girls of the neighborhood were insouciant in garish beach pajamas with hems measuring up to one hundred inches around. (Interestingly, both of these fads returned to popular vogue in the seventies.)

Unlike today, most of the older people did not copy the styles of the young but regarded these frivolities with disapproval, having apparently forgotten what it was like to be young and lighthearted. Their ceaseless preoccupation with practical concerns tended to discourage all freedom of expression and creativity.

Young people were expected — almost required — not to be "too sensitive." Sensitivity, which is now considered necessary to the higher development of humanity, was then thought of as a character flaw. A boy or girl who showed more interest in cultural than material pursuits ran the risk of being labeled a dreamer and misfit.

As previously noted, there was also a tendency on the part of some country people toward suspicion and bigotry. Although seldom actively hostile, there was an element among the backwoods folk who tended to keep their distance and to speak disparagingly of the newcomers and outsiders. This was no doubt due in large measure to the gnawing fears and frustrations of the times, for the harshness of life produced in some a corresponding harshness of spirit. This was demonstrated most overtly by the occasional savage brawlings of lumberjacks on Saturday night sprees, activities we heard about but seldom witnessed, since logging was less important in the Laurelhurst district than in some surrounding communities.

On the other hand, the people of our small district demonstrated the toughness and resiliency that humans are capable of achieving under stress. There was little overt covetousness and almost no stealing. No one really expected miraculous governmental salvation, despite promises from Washington of "a chicken in every pot." People learned to postpone, if not abandon, their aspirations. They dreamed wistfully over the Montgomery Ward catalog, universally known as "the wish book." With unexpected resourcefulness, they found ways to provide at small cost acceptable substitutes for the things they could not afford to buy.

The absence of a floor in her kitchen, for example, represented ultimate humiliation to Mom. As the years went by, we had our share of visitors, usually relatives from California and North Dakota and even some of the Ontario aristocrats from Dad's side of the family. The disgrace of entertaining in a floorless cave drove Mom nearly wild.

"When do I get my floor?" she raged one day for perhaps the hundredth time, knowing she might as well be asking for diamonds.

"I'll start it today," Dad answered calmly.

We all stared in disbelief, but Dad finished his coffee, packed and lit his pipe, and went out to the barn to hitch up the horses. Shortly before noon he returned with a wagonload of heavy planks, each about sixteen feet long and four by twelve inches in dimension. On one side, the planks showed signs of heavy wear, but the other side was smooth and scarcely even discolored.

These, it turned out, were the discarded planks from the McLeod bridge, which was undergoing a much-needed redecking by the Hartman Brothers of Jacksonville, pioneer bridge-builders of Jackson County. Dad had arranged with the Highway Department to get the old planking for the price of hauling it away. Smooth side up, these massive timbers looked as if they had just come from the mill instead of having withstood the rigors of traffic and weather for eighteen years. By contrast with the hard-packed pumice she had endured for five years, this floor was such a delight to Mom that she contented herself with it, uncovered by rug or linoleum, for the duration of our Rogue River stay.

THROUGH A FAVORABLE CONDITION of nature, the families living at the upper end of the Laurelhurst Loop tended to be more prosperous and to stay longer in the district than those of us at the lower end. The simple geological explanation for this fact was that the land improved and the water became more abundant as the bench sloped toward its upstream end. Beyond the upper limits of the district — that is, above the covered bridge — the gorge became too narrow and its slopes too steep to support agriculture or any other form of activity, but just below that point the benchland lay deep and rich in forest loam that was abundantly watered by many free-flowing springs high on the mountainside.

The original settlers — the Ditsworths, Peytons, and Vaughans — had recognized this fact back in the seventies and eighties and had taken up the choicest homestead sites and stayed on, generation after generation, to prosper there. At the lower end of the loop the soil was rocky and sterile, ranging from pumice deposits left from the long-past volcanic formation of Crater Lake to thin river sand. To add to our difficulties, the springs in our immediate vicinity were stingy and few. Thus, it was inevitable that the people of the upper Laurelhurst Loop would become employers and those in the lower district seekers after employment.

Aside from the endless chores at home — for which no young person in those days ever received an allowance — we were constantly on the alert for employment. Opportunities were rare and short-lived, however, and competition was intense. At first we three boys were too young to hire out as farm hands, so our only opportunity to earn money came from picking strawberries for the Ditsworths or the Richardsons.

The Ditsworth strawberries were of such fabulous quality that people still talk about them, thirty years after the last crop was harvested. Frank Ditsworth always denied that he ever insulted the virgin soil with commercial fertilizer, but Leo Hoag came upon him one day laying a thin streak of super phosphate along the rows. Embarrassed, Frank insisted that his young neighbor keep his secret. Even during the Depression, people drove many miles for the privilege of picking their own berries from the Ditsworth fields, but Frank never allowed them into the patch until the best of the crop had been gathered by his own pickers. On weekends in late June, as many as a hundred visitors lounged in their cars or in the shade of the great oaks, waiting for permission to "U-pick."

The season lasted about four weeks, from early June until just after the Fourth of July. During this time we toiled up and down the endless rows, dragging our carriers along and snipping the tough stems with stained fingernails. The sun burned our arms and backs. Strawberry picking is absorbing for a while, then tedious, and finally backbreaking. Growers usually close the fields in midafternoon because the mounting heat, strain, and monotony make the pickers careless. We started after the dew was dried from the plants and picked about six hours, with an hour off for lunch. When our crate felt about the right heft, we took it to the shed for weighing in. There, Frank's wife Maude presided as the pickers bustled back and forth.

The scales were impartial and so was Maude; if a crate was light, back it went for more berries, even if the picker's row happened to be two hundred yards away. Maude insisted that every cup be heaped with large red berries for top marketability. If any stems were torn out or any green fruit appeared, someone got a lesson in berry picking from the former schoolteacher, but she also made sure that the hired man made regular trips through the patch with the water bucket on hot afternoons. When opportunities arose — or even if they didn't — Frank lectured his youthful employees on the evils of "cigareets" and the Demon Rum. The Ditsworths were childless but over the years they became second parents to most of the youngsters within a fifteen-mile radius.

At the time we worked for them, the Ditsworths paid their pickers twenty-five cents for a clean, full-weight, twelve-cup crate, although earlier rates were as low as a penny a cup. An average picker could fill a crate in an hour, which I was seldom able to do. The younger married women, being more highly motivated, were somewhat faster than the kids, although eager youths like Darrell Nichols and Kenny Rogers regularly picked fifteen to eighteen crates a day, which was considered unbeatable.

Kenny, a competitive young swaggerer, sought to establish himself as field champion by challenging any newcomer who looked like a threat. When a buxom girl named May Green arrived and went to work, Kenny hastened to station himself in the row next to her and prepared to give her a berry-picking lesson. Taking no apparent notice of him, May, who picked standing spread-legged rather than kneeling like the others, simply walked away from him. At the end of the day, her tally was an unheard-of twenty-five crates!

Lunchtime was an occasion for social exchange as well as nourishment and physical relief. We munched our sandwiches under the shade trees by the great, rough-planked barn and furtively eyed the members of the opposite sex. Some of the girls looked as ripe as the strawberries. Snug-fitting jeans and gobs of lipstick accentuated their natural allure, and their sly glances and giggles stirred our adolescent blood. Bolder youths like my brother Danny and Dale Joliffe worked up enough courage to offer the prettier ones bicycle rides.

Later, as we resumed picking, the glances became more daring and the giggles and remarks more open. Sometimes a denim-clad bottom, looming at close range, was an irresistible target for a rotten strawberry. But Frank Ditsworth kept his eyes open for such shenanigans, and only the more daring among us were willing to take such risks.

One scorching hot afternoon, Bobby and I took an even greater gamble — and lost. Our shoulders ached, the picking was meager, and a nearby swimming hole beckoned. At length, able to bear it no longer, we ditched our carriers near the end of a row and circled around the field to where our bicycles were parked. Soon we were reveling in the cool water. The next morning Maude questioned us about our disappearance and soon wrung a confession from us. She then suggested we weren't old enough yet for the rigors of berry picking, and it dawned on us that we had been fired! Pedaling down the road, we felt, as Dad used to say, like the last rose of summer. Mom's unsympathetic reception when we arrived at home didn't help much.

The other major source of seasonal employment was the pear harvest at the Weeks orchard. Unlike berry picking, which was available to anyone over the age of ten, jobs in the pear harvest were generally limited to persons of high school age and above. A rather rigid form of sex discrimination was practiced in the harvesting and packing of tree fruits, although it did not always work to the advantage of the males.

Picking and general labor (distributing empties and collecting full lug boxes, loading, stacking, and cold storage) were men's duties, with picking compensated as piecework and general labor paid by the hour. Sorting and packing were women's jobs — the notable exception being the itinerant packers. Sorting was low-paid, monotonous work: separating fruit by size and grade. It, too, was paid on an hourly basis, about twenty-five cents per hour.

The only workers who could earn what might be considered big money were the packers, whose job was to wrap each pear in a square of thin, high-quality tissue and nest it in a precise geometric pattern in a box filled with precisely the same size and quality of fruit. This job called for skill, speed, and stamina, for the crew often worked ten- and twelve-hour days during the peak of the season. There was a strong bias in favor of women for this work, I suppose because it was thought to be a skill that came more naturally to women than to men.

If so, this presumption was not confirmed by the itinerant packers, or "fruit tramps," who were about equally divided between genders. Among them, men and women were very much on a par in skill and earning power. Growers tended to rely largely on itinerant packers for this critical function, as these nomads of the harvest developed great speed and skill by traveling constantly from crop to crop, starting with Arizona citrus in February and working their way gradually northward through the Washington apples in November. Unlike sorters, packers were paid by the box, and the speedy "fruit tramps" earned unbelievable sums by Depression standards. Even then, they drove Packards and Cadillacs and wore expensive clothes.

It was fascinating to watch the packers, hunched over the slanting packing stands, their bodies swaying rhythmically and their slim hands moving in a steady blur as the pillowed fruit rose steadily in the boxes before them. They were envied and admired for their skill, though not always respected, because their jaded faces and fancy clothes made them seem not quite proper to the threadbare local people. The more dexterous and determined of the local women — and a few men — managed to break the barrier and graduate from the humbler skills into packing.

Today, classes in fruit packing are conducted annually, so the growers are no longer dependent on itinerant workers. Back then, it took discernment for Stewart Weeks to see in young Erma Glass the natural athlete's coordination of hand and eye that would enable her to move directly from sorting to packing. Erma quickly demonstrated that she could pack pears as well as she could shoot baskets and hit home runs.

Out in the orchard, the pickers scaled their eighteen-foot ladders with canvas bags strapped to their shoulders, leaving each tree only when the last pear was garnered, no matter the peril required to capture it. When the bag was full, the picker descended the ladder, released the snap-fastened canvas bottom of his picking bag, and eased the hard, green pears into a lug box. Picking being piecework, there was no time for more than a quick stretch to ease aching shoulders before setting and remounting the ladder. Throughout the day, flatbed trucks crawled the rutted orchard rows, picking up full boxes and taking them to the cold storage plant.

Experiments have since been conducted in picking mechanically — some have even tried using grotesquely elongated stilts to eliminate the need for ladders — but the only real change in picking technology since the thirties is the replacement of the lug box, capacity about forty pounds, with huge cubical plywood containers, four feet on each side, which are loaded mechanically. Today, the old lug boxes are valuable antiques and may be seen as display cases in the quaint shops of Jacksonville and Ashland.

A boy could get a picking job at fourteen if he was husky enough. We all eventually got our turns at this most arduous of harvest tasks, but while I was still too small I heard of a special job in the Weeks orchard so appealing that I would have taken it without pay. It was said that, prior to the harvest, Mr. Weeks engaged a man to shoot the downy woodpeckers that infested his trees, since these birds liked to vary their diet of bugs — to which they would have been welcome — with an occasional pear. It was reliably reported that the orchardist paid a bounty of ten cents for every woodpecker shot on his property. Overcoming my shyness, I made the four-mile trip by bicycle and found Mr. Weeks in the vast packing shed. He listened to my faltering application.

"How old are you, Wallace?" he asked kindly.

"Ten," I told him.

He smiled gently. "I'm afraid that's a little young for the job. Besides, I already have a man out there shooting those birds. I wouldn't want two of you shooting back and forth; somebody might get hit."

Thus I missed my only chance to become a professional hunter.

During these hardest times, there was never enough money. Even to feed the cows, chickens, and turkeys, our parents had to scrounge for credit, and these short-term accommodations had to be repaid immediately from the next pittance Dad earned in his brief and infrequent periods of employment. This chronic shortage was particularly demoralizing to Mom, though she usually concealed her sagging spirits from us. Once, though, I glimpsed how apt was the term "depression."

A favorite strategy of mine to get out of washing the evening dishes was to feign sleep after dinner, hoping Mom would take pity on me and do it herself. Occasionally it worked. One night I was reclining in my favorite position against the woodpile behind the stove. Danny and Bobby had already gone out to do their evening chores, and Mom and Dad lingered at the table talking. My ruse must have been successful, for their conversation turned abruptly serious. While Dad puffed on his old "nose warmer," Mom stared morosely out the kitchen window.

"Look at us," she lamented. "Two intelligent, hard-working people, and what have we got to show for all this work? Nothing! We're falling farther behind instead of getting ahead!" She dabbed at her tears with her apron and her voice fell to a whisper of despair. "We might just as well jump in the river and float away!"

Dad gave her a long, searching look, then patted her hand gently. Such a gesture of tenderness was rare for him.

"This is going to work out all right, Sig," he said quietly. "You'll see."

His response had a wonderfully calming effect on Mom. She managed a tremulous smile and began collecting the dishes.

At the first opportunity I scooted out the kitchen door.

chapter nine

Rustic pleasures

TO OUR BOYISH MINDS, the word "depression" was associated only with the prevailing economic condition; it had little to do with the state of our spirits. Living so close to nature in a land of scenic splendor and benign climate, having access without cost to so many of the necessities if few of the luxuries of life, it was impossible to dwell very long on our misfortunes, especially when we had so much company. My brothers and I, like the mountain men of a century earlier, felt as if we owned the world.

The four seasons were sharply distinct, each bringing its special joys. In winter we went sledding on the hill alongside the house, bouncing over the ruin of an ancient ditch and soaring almost to the flatland below. Freezing weather produced sheet ice, a foot thick and clear as window glass, on the long, narrow, sheltered pool that lay in the lee of one of the three large islands adjacent to our property. Stuffing the toes of our parents' skates with cotton, we would take turns skimming the transparent surface until long after dark. Beneath us the stones of the channel were as clearly visible as the bare alder branches overhead.

Once, we found the perfectly preserved body of a huge bald eagle frozen in the ice. We deduced that while the ice was still thin he had stooped for a fish and stunned himself against the unexpected barrier, which first shattered under the impact and then sealed the great bird — by then dead or crippled — in its grip.

In our exhilaration, we didn't even want to go home for supper. Instead we broiled strips of venison over a fire on the edge of the ice. It was usually nine or ten o'clock when we finally trudged home, picking out the dim trail by the light of the stars.

Often I would wake at night with the winter moon shining in on our open porch. At such times the familiar world about us was transformed into a fairyland. Icicles three and four feet long fringed the overhanging roof. Rabbits, lost in their own world of nocturnal play, scampered on the flat below. The fir towered like a sentinel over our little house, and snow formed soft hummocks on the hazelnut clumps. Often the coyotes yapped their shrill serenade from the hills above. So precious were these moments that I begrudged sleep and only gave up my vigil when finally overwhelmed by drowsiness.

Spring usually came early, spreading its soft green stain across meadow and mountain. Wildflowers sprang up everywhere — bluebonnets and tiger lilies, skunk cabbages and yellow daisies. Wild strawberries mantled the hills, and the fragrance of mingled bloom scented the woods. Fat, arrogant jays scolded raucously and meadowlarks warbled on the flat below the house. Downy woodpeckers noisily drilled the curling bark of cherry and apple trees and their cousins, the enormous pileated woodpeckers of the deep forest, made rare appearances. Mushrooms festooned the meadows, the skeletal

75

oaks burst into leaf, and soft gray buds adorned the willows.

Restless from the constraints of winter and sensing the burgeoning of life around us, we ran wild when spring arrived. At
every spare moment I was off in the woods with my Stevens
.22-caliber single-shot rifle, harassing the jays, squirrels, and
rabbits. As the days grew warmer, I climbed Jim Mann Hill, the
promontory above our house, and simply dreamt the hours away
watching the buzzards and eagles soar in the blue sky or the
ant-sized cars toiling up the Crater Lake Highway far below,
across the river. At other times, standing on a low hill ablaze
with flowers while the wind streamed against my face, I became
so intoxicated with the wine of spring that I felt an overpowering
need to yell out loud for the sheer joy of being alive.

One fine day when the spirit of adventure lured me far beyond
the brow of Jim Mann Hill — normally the boundary of my
travels — I found myself following a dim but level path through
a forest of immense firs and pines. For no known reason, I probed
deeper and deeper into this new territory until sounds of human
activity came to my ears. Astonished, I pressed on and soon
came to the edge of a clearing. There stood a log house and barn,
and in a nearby corral two men were shoeing a horse. I watched
silently, unobserved, for twenty minutes or so, then withdrew
like an alien invader in a forbidden country. At home, my parents knew nothing of such a place or any road penetrating the
area where I had been and were half inclined to think that I had
imagined the whole thing.

On another occasion, I discovered a small ghost town, if
"town" is an appropriate description for a cluster of shacks,
numbering possibly half a dozen, plus a few small outbuildings.
I had been following an overgrown dirt road, dimly visible
among the alder saplings sprouting in its tracks, through a
gloomy wood not far from the place where our flume leaped the
ravine below Rumley Creek. It looked no different from any
abandoned logging road and, finding the going difficult and the
lonely setting a trifle oppressive, I was at the point of turning
back when I came upon the small settlement. There was even
what could be called a street running between two rows of tiny
one-roomed shanties.

Planks creaked and hinges groaned as I pushed my way into
first one and then another of the deserted buildings. Nothing

remained in any of them but pole bunks, rude tables, and a few rusty skillets and coffee pots. The walls were covered with old newspapers, now stained and shredded by packrats. I stared curiously at an ancient headline: "War Looms in Europe." The paper was dated in 1913, six years before I was born. To this day I have not found another person who ever saw the deserted hamlet or could explain the mystery of its departed inhabitants.

Shortly after the first wildflowers became evident, livestock from the lower valley began to appear, marking the beginning of the grazing season. Beef cattle and a few horses roamed the hills around us. Strangely enough, though, the event that stirred us most was the arrival of the sheep. We came to know almost to the day when to expect them, and we listened intently for the sound of the approaching flock. Then it came, the distant bleating of a thousand voices from the direction of the river road.

Before the sheep actually came into sight, the canvas-covered chuck wagon rounded the bend, making its way to the annual campsite on the flat just north of our house. The cook liked to make camp before the herdsmen arrived with their horses, dogs, and the flock. By the time the chuck wagon passed our house the bleating was much louder, and soon the first animals appeared. Moments later the hillside was alive with a moving mass of sheep. Their "baah-baah-baahs" grew steadily louder as the entire flock moved into view. Sheep have a clear, penetrating cry and on the move make an amazing racket for such gentle creatures. Over the bleating we could hear the occasional shouting of the herdsmen and the constant yelping of the collies, moving ceaselessly with the uncanny knowingness of all sheepdogs. The drivers worked stragglers and strays into the main mass and moved the entire flock steadily up the road, giving no apparent signals as they swayed to the zig-zagging of the horses.

We knew that the leaders had already reached the campground by the time the last of the sheep disappeared. We hurried through supper and followed them, timing our arrival to coincide with the disappearance of the last daylight, for we always liked to visit the sheep camp when the herdsmen were lounging about the campfire, their evening meal finished and their big tin coffee cups before them. They seemed to look forward to these meetings too and always greeted us cordially.

Naturally taciturn like many outdoorsmen, their conversation was sparse and low-keyed. They communicated chiefly through the motionless hunch of the shoulders, the slow turning of the head, the faint crooked smile, and the languid lifting of the coffee cup. Each man's eyes fixed on the hypnotic, dancing flames while his thoughts roamed. The stars crept out to light the velvet sky. The sheep, seen dimly as they bedded down among the meager pines, were quiet now, seldom breaking the evening stillness.

As the fire burned low, we realized the lateness of the hour and headed reluctantly down the hill toward home. Next morning the school bus would push its way through the herd, already on the move toward the summer grazing ground high on the mountainside.

Strangely enough, there were two small streams with the same name — Lost Creek — both entering the Rogue at almost the same place, but on opposite sides of the river. On the Crater Lake Highway side, across from us, a plain little meadow brook meandered through the pastures of the Carleton ranch. The other Lost Creek, the one on the Laurelhurst side, tumbled out of the Rogue River Mountains through dense stands of Douglas fir and cedar in a series of bubbling, crystalline pools. It entered the Rogue on the old Brophy property, about a mile north of our place, cascading down a wooded slope so remote that its exact location was unknown to most of us. In contrast to its undistinguished twin, this Lost Creek was a matchless jewel, a charmed place that cast an enduring spell over those who came to know it.

All winter long we looked forward to fishing Lost Creek in the spring, for we knew that large numbers of trout entered it from the river at this time and made their way upstream as far as Lost Creek Falls. This knowledge was a secret well kept by the kids, who were aware that the sportsmen from the lower valley normally concentrated their attention on the main river. One fine Saturday in April four of us — Jim Thomas, Kenny Rogers, Danny, and I — met at our place and hiked up to Lost Creek. Our gear was light — a tobacco tin of worms, a roll of cuddyhunk line, a few snelled hooks, and a sandwich. We would cut poles later when we reached the stream.

Arriving at the place where Lost Creek ran under the road, we were tempted to try the basin below the culvert, but none of us would give the others first chance at the main prize, the big pool below the falls. We all struck off upstream, following a deer trail bordering the stream. Tall cedars and firs stood along the way, and drooping ferns nearly concealed the path. Many a foaming pool diverted our attention. It was torture to pass them up, but on we plunged, each trying to be first to our destination.

Finally, after nearly a mile, a steady roar drowned the lesser murmuring of the stream. We resisted as unsportsmanlike the desire to break into a run, but each of us stretched his stride a little. Then the coveted place was before us, the goal of our long winter dreams. A twenty-foot cataract plunged into a pool of perhaps the same diameter. A rocky ledge, just wide enough to stand on, skirted one side of the pool and a gravel beach the other. A huge log, heavy with moss, stood on its end in the water and leaned against the rim of the falls. The thundering cataract drowned out our excited chatter. The air about us sparkled with spray.

Nervously, we rigged our gear and baited up. Almost at once there was a yell, and a twelve-inch trout flopped on the gravel. Then another of almost the same size. After twenty minutes or so, this furious action slackened, and with a dozen fish already caught, we worked our way down into the lower pools.

We finished that day with sixty-five trout, ranging from seven to twelve inches. The larger ones had nearly all come from the pool below the falls. Not wanting to leave, we explored the site of a moonshiner's still and the ruin of a burned-out sawmill near the culvert. At last, and only out of the necessity of keeping our fish from spoiling, we turned our footsteps down the winding road toward home.

As soon as school was out, we threw away our worn-out shoes and joyfully greeted the new summer with bare feet. Within a week those same feet looked as if they had never known shoes. Tough, dark hide, like the pads of a wolf, covered the soles and protected us from stubble and thorn. Only the ends of the toes were vulnerable: a stubbed toe, I recall, is one of the most painful injuries to which a barefoot boy is prone.

Once chores were finished each day, we could roam as far as energy and imagination dictated, for our parents, unlike most of the neighbors, believed in giving us free reign. Actually, Dad was too preoccupied to oversee us; it was Mom who conceived the notion that freedom would make us self-reliant. However,

79

there were many occurrences, of which she knew nothing at the time, that put her theory to the severest test. We fell from trees, got bucked off horses, plummeted through barn lofts, nearly drowned in the river, trod among rattlesnakes, walked bridge trestles, dove from cliffs, got lost in the mountains, slid down haystacks, stepped on rusty nails, played with firearms, and sometimes fought each other like savages.

Several times before I was thirteen I waded Rogue River, a dangerous undertaking even for a full-grown man equipped with felt-soled waders. Each time, before I reached midstream the current swept me off my feet, and I bobbed like a chip in the turbulent rapids. Fortunately I didn't panic and swallow water, so I eventually reached slack water, where I could get my footing and wade ashore. After one of these adventures, when I arrived half drowned at McLeod store — still clutching my fishing pole despite emerging from the river a quarter-mile below my starting point — Mr. Hoag reported the incident to Mom and warned her that none of us would live long enough to vote if she didn't keep us out of that river! But our mother, who was and still is a woman of great religious faith, continued to entrust our safety to the Lord, and he showed his faithfulness, for none of us ever suffered so much as a broken bone.

Summer was a time of picnicking, the weather being predominantly fine but overly hot for indoor dining. Dad built a picnic table and set it in the shade of a grove of trees near the river. Each day, when we went to get water, we set jars of milk, crocks of food, and perhaps a watermelon in the river pools, trapping them with rocks to prevent them from floating away. In the heat of the late afternoon we went to this cool retreat for supper and stayed, skipping flat stones across the river and wading by the gravelly beach, until bedtime.

On the Fourth of July, we launched skyrockets and Roman candles out over the water. These and other fireworks we earned by selling subscriptions to the *Oregon Farmer Magazine*.

For several summers Dad obtained employment as head boatman at Diamond Lake resort, where he rented boats and motors, sold fishing tackle, and answered foolish questions about where the fish were likely to be found. We joined him for two or three weeks each season, camping in a tent and offering him a token of home life while enjoying a vacation ourselves.

Surprisingly, after a few days, time hung heavy and we were glad to forsake the tepid pleasures of resort life to return to our own wild haunts. One long and boring afternoon — I was nine or ten at the time — Dad let me take out a rowboat, and I decided to row the length of the lake. Diamond Lake, I later learned, is about five miles long, and that waterlogged hulk was not a racing shell. Doggedly, I tugged on the oars and measured the infinitesimally small progress of each stroke by the gradually shifting positions of cabins and trees. The sun sank lower in the sky; still I pulled, thinking each bend in the shoreline would surely open upon my destination. Dusk came, and finally I could see, a half mile distant, the reedy marshland at the south end of the lake.

It dawned on me then that I had to repeat every single pull on those wretched oars in order to get back to the resort, and I quickly reversed directions. The sun set behind Mount Thielsen, stars broke out in the evening sky, and campfires winked along the shoreline; still I rowed monotonously on. It was nearly ten o'clock when I finally made out the dim shape of my mother standing on the end of the dock, doubting for once, I imagine, the wisdom of parental permissiveness. But because her relief was greater than her wrath, I escaped to bed weary but unspanked.

A MAJOR EVENT in our lives was the appearance of "company," especially visitors who came to stay for a time. Visits lasting several weeks were not uncommon, and we delighted in showing off the wonders of our rustic environment to these outsiders.

An unvarying and always successful practical joke to initiate any visitor was to toss him a basketball-sized chunk of pumice — which could be found almost anywhere — with the unexpected command, "Catch it!" Outwardly looking much like any rugged fieldstone, these "pummey rocks," as we called them, were blobs of volcanic foam spewed across the landscape during the cataclysmic formation of Crater Lake. They were soft and gritty to the touch, pinkish beige in color, and nearly weightless. After the "Catch it!" game, we always threw one of the larger chunks in the river and enjoyed our guests' expressions of astonishment at seeing a "rock" float.

One day early in the summer of 1932 the mailman brought a letter that produced great excitement in our household. Dad's youngest brother Frank, of whom we had often heard Dad speak, wrote from South Africa to say that he was relocating in western Canada and would like to visit us en route. It was a long and somewhat autobiographical letter, since much had happened to its author since his last communication with his favorite brother.

Dad filled in as best he could what the letter left out. Frank had left wartime employment in a Toronto bank at seventeen to enlist in the Royal Canadian Air Force and flew many sorties against the Germans before he was eventually shot down over France. He was captured immediately and spent the remaining year and a half of World War I in a German prison camp. When the war ended, he was released to a hero's welcome in London, which included a madcap romance that culminated in his marriage to a British heiress.

Suddenly his fortunes were reversed by the discovery of tuberculosis in his spine, the result of his prison privations. A series of treatments, operations, and convalescences in several famous sanatoriums followed, lasting more than a decade. In these places, the young Canadian, who possessed great charm and a quick, inquiring mind, made good use of his enforced idleness by cultivating the acquaintance of good books and cultured, well-educated patients. In Switzerland, France, and South Africa, his stubborn spinal infection slowly yielded to rest and treatment. Now, after many years of confinement and nearly a score of operations, his infection, though not healed, had become sealed in a calcified cyst, and his general health was improved to the point where his discharge was considered safe. Unhappily, his marriage had dissolved under the stress of these difficulties, and he hoped to make a new life in Victoria, capital city of British Columbia, on Vancouver Island.

Dad, who was normally the least demonstrative of men, responded to the news of his brother's impending visit with great enthusiasm. He immediately constructed a tent-house in the shade of the huge cherry trees where the old Toney house had stood. Then, casting frugality to the winds, he rolled the old Stevens off its blocks in the barn and cleaned it up for Frank's personal use. Accustomed as we had become to regarding the formless, shrouded shape as permanently inert, we stared in awe at its reborn beauty and marveled at the powerful roar of its engine. The sisters of Lazarus could scarcely have been more astonished at his resurrection than we at the sight of the risen Stevens.

The day of our celebrated uncle's arrival finally came. We fidgeted on the station platform in Medford as the locomotive steamed and a handful of passengers disembarked. Dad, scanning each face, abruptly broke forward to greet a handsome, smiling, well-groomed man, remarkably similar in looks to himself though much younger and decidedly cosmopolitan. We stared at the rough Harris tweed jacket, creased gray flannel trousers, and polished brown oxfords. Our uncle greeted each of us by name without needing introductions and enlivened the homeward journey with gay anecdotes and lively chatter about the places he had been and things he had done.

Uncle Frank settled into the tent-house while we marveled at the wealth of his wardrobe and accoutrements and pestered him with questions about his war experiences. He treated us with great kindliness and civility and, as the summer wore on, shared generously of his glamorous background, so strange and exotic to our ears. He was a gifted raconteur and loved an audience. His presence in the locality was quickly discovered by the valley socialites, who pressed him with invitations to speak at teas and ladies' club meetings.

When none of these engagements claimed his time, it was his custom to linger over his breakfast coffee and talk expansively to any members of the family who happened to be there to hear. Because of the press of chores and other interests, this usually came down to Mom and me — Mom because her duties kept her in the kitchen at this time of day and me because I couldn't have been dragged away. Through hero worship on my part and appreciation of a good listener on his, we became the best of comrades that summer. As he talked, a world of hitherto unknown splendor opened up to me, a world of kings and archdukes, popes and generals, poets, authors, courtesans, knaves, adventurers, and savages. Cockney slang, Swahili dialect, Parisian argot, Irish brogue — all tumbled easily from his lips.

While this cataract of brilliance eddied about her, Mom bustled about her kitchen, turning Frank's monologue on and off as her interest and physical proximity directed. As for me, I never missed a syllable. Because of his years of stimulating conversation and reading Uncle Frank was astoundingly knowledgeable, not only in current affairs but in historical events, and he seldom faltered for a word. Once while discussing the assassination of Czar Nicholas and his family, he hesitated, searching for the name of the assassin of Rasputin, the sinister, half-mad monk.

"Yousapouf," I supplied, interjecting my first word of the day. The Hearst editorials had finally paid off!

Uncle Frank accepted this assistance, stared at me briefly, then continued his discourse. Mom sailed about the kitchen, planning her day and barely attending these pearls of erudition.

Uncle Frank spent the entire summer and early fall of 1932 with us. Despite his popularity with the society ladies of Medford — a source of anguish and jealousy to me — he devoted long hours to his hillbilly nephews, sharing our swimming hole at Big Butte Creek, taking us sightseeing, and treating us to movies and chocolate milkshakes. We wanted him to stay forever, but his adopted son Gordon, who was spending the summer with his mother in Switzerland, was soon to be entered into school in Victoria, and this duty brought to an end the most memorable of my Rogue River summers. As I hung about the tent-house watching him pack, it seemed to me that the dazzling world I had glimpsed so briefly was also being folded up and tucked away forever in the polished leather luggage.

WITH FALL came not only a return to school but a resumption of what little social activity took place in the community. These events usually occurred either at Hoag's McLeod store or at the Laurelhurst schoolhouse. The ladies of the neighborhood did their best to sustain some community life, however modest and irregular. Halloween parties, box socials, and Christmas plays were well attended by young and old.

In addition, the livelier folk took in the Saturday night dances at Rogue Elk resort, which featured twangy, sentimental music and an occasional fist fight. Early in the 1930s a local Grange chapter was organized, and this agency afforded social expression, exchange of farming information, and a forum through which members attempted to influence politicians.

Religious worship occurred spasmodically, varying with the zeal of its organizers. Sunday school — it was never called church — was a nondenominational activity well attended by women and younger children and by a scattering of men. The service consisted primarily of singing, it being difficult to find laymen who would — or could — preach and impossible to negotiate more than one or two visits a year by a real minister. Nevertheless, we sang with great fervor, and I warmly recall those meetings whenever I hear old hymns like "Bringing in the Sheaves" and "Work, for the Night is Coming."

Dad routinely excused himself from Sunday worship service with the explanation that he had "graduated" from Sunday school. Mom also absented herself much of the time, preferring private devotions, but she insisted that we attend, and once the habit was formed we needed little urging. When Sunday school was held at the Laurelhurst school we made the five-mile trip on our bicycles.

One October Sunday after service, while pedaling home along a level stretch near the site of the original log schoolhouse above Lost Creek, we were startled to see a large buck deer trotting up the road toward us. His attention seemed to be focused on something behind him; he had apparently been flushed by hunters in the hills above.

It was only when the distance between the deer and us had narrowed to fifteen feet or so that he became aware of our presence; then he veered off the road, leaped the wire fence at roadside, and crossed a weed-choked field. At its far side, just short of the trees, another fence obstructed his escape. The buck bounded over this obstacle too but failed to clear the strand of barbed wire above it. He fell on his back, one foreleg tangled between the barbed wire and the woven fencing.

We quickly dismounted and ran to the place where the deer lay caught. So firmly was he imprisoned that there was clearly no chance of his escape; nevertheless, we had heard enough stories of the perils of a deer's hooves to make us approach warily. Danny whipped out his pocket knife and, while I held the antlers, sliced through the jugular. As the struggle slackened, we sent Bobby to bring our father; then Danny and I disengaged the tangled leg and dragged the heavy body to the roadside, negotiating the second fence just as Dad arrived with the truck.

This story appeared on the front page of the *Medford Mail Tribune* and included a gratuitous comment by the reporter about divine rewards for Sunday school attendance. We were pleased enough by this publicity but grateful that some of our other hunting exploits went unreported.

chapter ten
High school

BY THE TIME Danny and I completed our elementary school education in 1932, the Laurelhurst school board had finally recognized the futility of maintaining a high school that never attracted more than seven or eight pupils. Reluctantly, they closed
the high school and considered the alternatives. The county
school superintendent informed the board members that they
could either transport us to Prospect, then about fifteen miles
away, or enroll us at Butte Falls High, about twice that distance,

and arrange for us to be boarded there. This choice was presented to the parents of the affected young people. Mom and Dad decided on Prospect, as did most of the others.

Mr. Harding, whose two daughters, Dorothy and Maxine, were of high school age, was hired to drive from his place on Butte Creek up the Laurelhurst road, picking up Erma and Lois Glass, Tommy Close, Danny, and me along the way. He deposited us at the Flounce Rock Ranch on the winding Crater Lake Highway, where we waited to be picked up by the Prospect school bus. The daily round trip required something over two hours.

When we entered high school at Prospect, Danny and I had seen this picturesque mountain hamlet perhaps three or four times previously, although we had been living on the Upper Rogue for six years. Once again we felt like aliens.

The visitor to Prospect, now as well as then, senses something different about the place, an aura of the frontier despite the blatantly visible trappings of the twentieth century. One has the feeling of being at the outer edge of civilization, a short step from primal wilderness. In the thirties this impression was not altogether illusory, but it was only much later that I learned Prospect's nearly forgotten story.

In 1872, two pioneers named Slawson and Beeson followed a dim forest trail over the Rogue River Mountains until they arrived at a place so captivating that they proceeded to unload their wagons and establish a sawmill on the spot.

Soon others were attracted by the opportunity for employment, and a raw frontier settlement sprang up on the rocky banks of the narrow, turbulent Upper Rogue. They called the little hamlet Tail Hold for reasons now lost. Some say that a timber wolf prowled the settlement one night and stole a puppy from a cabin porch. The cabin dweller allegedly ran out and saved the puppy by seizing the marauder by the tail, but this version is understandably disputed. A more likely explanation is that the inhabitants, believing themselves at the outer edge of the planet, chose a name that rudely suggested that impression.

After a devastating mill fire, the partners sold out in 1876 to a versatile entrepreneur named Deskins, who combined a lucrative business of stealing timber with the delivery of illicit firewater to the Indians of the new Fort Klamath reservation. After flourishing for a time, Deskins overreached himself by volunteering to "go out" for the community's winter supplies, only to return with his wagons loaded with whiskey instead of food and dry goods. His furious and panic-stricken fellow-townsmen, sensing early winter in the chill October wind, listened dubiously as Deskins explained his plan to triple their investment with one last quick trip to the reservation. But the glib tongue prevailed, and Deskins struck out over the mountains with a companion named Friel.

After camping at the summit, the two men woke to find themselves snowed in by an early blizzard and unable to proceed or retreat with the loaded wagons. They considered their problem while sampling the cargo and decided to sacrifice the contents of the barrels to a nearby stream, thereby bestowing upon it the lasting name of Whiskey Creek. Deskins then fled the region forever. The subsequent sufferings of the Tail Hold settlers were intensified when the river rose and tore out the bridge that connected them so precariously to the outside world.

The enterprising Deskins was succeeded by a solid, upright Vermonter named Stanford Aiken, who, as a Jacksonville storekeeper, had recently established a modest place in the history of southern Oregon by introducing the nickel into the inflated economy of that gold-glutted city. "Squire" Aiken, as he was respectfully called by his neighbors, bought the Tail Hold sawmill holdings from the deserted Mary Deskins and relocated operations to a nearby site less vulnerable to the whims of the river.

Aiken and others envisioned that the little mill town would one day become a major rail center for the shipment of lumber to Medford and Fort Klamath, a hope for the future they publicly declared by naming the new location "Prospect." All that was lacking was a railroad. Unfortunately, the Southern Pacific Railroad officials did not see the same possibilities and never got around to laying the hundred miles or so of track through the rugged mountains that would have brought this dream to fruition, so Prospect's prospects failed to materialize.

(To this day many residents are under the impression that the town got its name from early gold mining operations, which indeed flourished in other parts of Jackson County. But the prevailing geological structure in the Prospect area is igneous

89

rock and pumice, which were spewed forth by Mount Mazama at the time Crater Lake was created. This substance, enriched by many centuries of forest duff, produces magnificent evergreen trees but is innocent of any trace of precious metals.)

At the time we entered high school there, the town centered around the school, the big log store, and the Prospect Hotel. The latter included a cluster of rustic cabins rented by school-teachers, itinerant workers, and summer vacationers. A post office, a gas station and garage, and twelve to fifteen cottage homes made up the remainder of the community.

The Prospect High School faculty consisted of Ray Zobel, who was principal, teacher, and coach; Mrs. Frances Pearson, the widowed daughter of town founder Squire Aiken; and Pat Nichols, the jolly young bride of Darrell Nichols, the demon berry picker of my young working days. During our years at Prospect High, the student body consistently numbered about thirty-five pupils for all four grades.

Although I did reasonably well scholastically at Prospect after overcoming the shock of our transition from the primitive Laurelhurst school, my recollections of the classroom are re-markably sketchy. I do remember the fascination of exploring the great log store across the street during noon hours and squandering an occasional nickel on an ice cream cone at the marble-topped fountain. And there were severe attacks of spring fever as I contemplated a drift of snow, as high as a man's head, melting under the eaves of the store and listened to the clang of horseshoes thrown by the seasonally idled loggers when I should have been attending the pedantic dronings of "Profes-sor" Zobel. (For some reason, all rural high school principals were accorded the honorary if undeserved title of professor.)

Then there were the logging trucks that rumbled through town with huge loads of Douglas fir and sugar pine logs. In the fall we gawked at the red-hatted hunters who stopped to refresh themselves and show off big buck deer strapped across the hoods of their cars.

But my strongest and fondest association with Prospect has to do with discovering basketball, a game that has become a lifelong love. In those times basketball easily dominated other athletic events, probably because it was usually possible for even the smallest schools to find enough athletes for a five-man game, whereas many could never have fielded a complete baseball or football team. Before the consolidation of small rural school districts came into general practice, this condition prevailed in many parts of the nation.

One small but high-powered midwestern school with a total male enrollment of five won the state championship despite the fact that one member of the team was nearsighted and totally uncoordinated. In order to satisfy the rule requiring five players to be on the floor at all times, the coach issued standing orders to the nonathlete to stay clear of the action and to the others to avoid committing fouls at all costs.

Another tiny wonder-team of that era achieved the same distinction even though they played their first indoor games at the state tournament. When asked what adjustments they had to make in playing in a real gymnasium, they declared it had been easy and exclaimed, "We didn't even have to allow for the wind!"

The old Prospect gymnasium had a single row of benches along the sides. The lighting and heating arrangements, as I recall, were above average for those days — at Sams Valley, midway between Prospect and Medford, the gym received inadequate warmth from a potbellied stove that actually projected onto the playing floor and had to be kept constantly in mind during play. One subzero night when we were playing there, the referee had to whistle time out to remove his shoes and rub enough circulation into his half-frozen toes to continue.

When I played, basketball bore little resemblance to the fast-breaking, innovative game that it has become. Only two techniques were permitted for shooting field goals: the two-hand set shot, with both feet planted firmly on the floor, and the running push shot, using the right hand only.

Foul shots were always executed in the underhand style, and ball control was considered more important than scoring. No one paid any attention to the clock; in fact, the only person able to determine the official time was the timekeeper. No athlete, either in high school or in college, was ever known to "stuff" a basketball downward through the hoop, and though it was not illegal, the few players of that era who possessed the leg spring necessary to accomplish this feat would never have dreamed of trying anything so unconventional. But tall youths by the thousands, some still in junior high school, routinely "dunk" baskets today.

Although scores were low and the action rather mild compared to today's game, nearly everyone in the community turned out for the Friday night contests and would have been disappointed to see fewer than three or four games — usually boys' first and second teams, girls' team, and the town team. The latter consisted of local loggers and teachers, who sometimes continued to compete into their forties.

In our second year at Prospect High, the school's basketball fortunes received a much-needed stimulus from Bert Broomfield, a lanky youth whose family had recently arrived from San Francisco. Broomfield moved with the supple grace of a cat and displayed feats of ball-handling and shooting that none of us had ever seen before. Coming off a three-game losing streak, the team went on with Bert's help to win the last four regular season games and to place high in the southern Oregon tournament at Ashland, where Bert easily won the most valuable player award. He was offered an athletic scholarship, but had decided on a logging career and wasn't interested in college.

Every small town needs — and most of them have — a "character" to add color and zest to the measured tempo of village life. Before, during, and long after our scholastic tenure there, Prospect boasted such a figure in the hulking person of Dewey Hill, who later came to be known by nearly everyone in southern Oregon. He would have been about thirty-four when we arrived, for a Mrs. Pearson, our history teacher (who is now in her nineties and still keen of wit), remarked to me recently, "It is not very hard to trace the age of anyone who was named after the hero of Manila Bay."

Dewey was big, loud, jovial, blustering, profane, and thoroughly likable. He had never married and appeared to spend all his time in pursuit of big game, mirth, and athletic glory. His cabin was impressively adorned with hides and antlers. He dressed like any logger and may, intermittently, have been one. In winter he played center on the town basketball team. The sight and sound of Dewey charging down the floor, snorting like a bull elk and bellowing instructions to his teammates, remains forever stamped in my memory. In summer he acted as catcher and manager of the Prospect baseball team. Once, having identified a need for a southpaw in his pitching rotation, he encouraged me to play and even coached me for a time, but baseball was never my game so the experiment failed.

Dewey cultivated the reputation of an invincible backwoods wrestler and succeeded in implanting this image in the minds of most of his fellows. When truckers paused for refreshments or loggers stomped into the store, where he customarily lounged on sunny days, Dewey greeted them with ribald insults and invited them to meet him in the school gym across the street. The usual response was a grin that acknowledged this to be more a pleasantry than a threat, and most considered it something of a compliment as well.

As a brief diversion from the usual six months of continuous basketball, somebody once organized a smoker featuring boxing, wrestling, and tumbling. It was to be climaxed by a wrestling match between the redoubtable Dewey Hill and Mr. Zobel, who had been a varsity heavyweight wrestler in college. I contributed insignificantly to this smoker by getting punched out on my feet by Louie Jantzer, who was twenty-five pounds heavier and much more aggressive than I. Dewey served as my corner man and, by liberal applications of smelling salts, kept me going until the bell at the end of the third and final round put a merciful end to the slaughter.

When the headline attraction was announced, all the men and boys hitched their chairs forward expectantly. Mr. Zobel, who was then about thirty-five, looked pink, fit, and formidable in his college wrestling tights. Dewey, bare-chested and hairy, was about the same size and appeared for all the world the frontier champion he considered himself to be. Snorting fiercely and pawing the air with his big-knuckled woodsman's hands, he circled the crouching principal. When the two opponents finally closed and locked arms about each other's torso, the audience whooped and whistled.

The two big men strained at each other for perhaps a full minute, then banged down together on the mat. The impact of their fall was accompanied by three sounds so close together they were almost one — a thud, a loud crack, and an agonized scream. Then Ray Zobel rolled clear and rested on one knee while Dewey Hill writhed on the canvas and clutched at a broken rib. This, of course, ended the match but left the question of supremacy unresolved.

Dewey's self-esteem recovered along with the fractured rib, and by the time it was whole again he was telling everyone who would listen what dreadful things he would have done to "the perfesser" had misfortune not robbed him of the opportunity. Among the skeptics was Danny, who weighed about 145 pounds and was becoming a pretty fair wrestler himself. Moreover, he never took a dare, then or later, and when Dewey hurled a perfunctory challenge his way, Danny surprised even himself by taking the big mountaineer down and sitting on him. In that proud moment my brother believed he had arrived at a man's estate.

The old Prospect Hotel had been built in 1892 by a man named Boothby. Its business grew with the creation of Crater Lake National Park by President Theodore Roosevelt in 1909 and, as a result, the development of the Crater Lake Highway, which was built by convict labor in 1911.

When the highway was surfaced with macadam in 1919, the hotel's business really began to boom. Hordes of Californians, not yet accustomed to the novelty of the automobile and also eager to experience what the local promoters were billing as the Eighth Wonder of the World (that is, Crater Lake), streamed up the new highway. Many stopped at the Prospect Hotel for meals and lodging.

Although the Depression (which some say extended from 1929 to 1934 but, by southern Oregon's experience, was not really over until 1938 or '39) tended to slow the flow of tourists somewhat, the old hotel still did a respectable business. During that period an affable gentleman named Jim Grieve operated both the hotel and the adjacent cluster of rustic cabins, which were scattered beneath the great firs and cedars along the wild and beautiful Red Blanket Creek. Set among the timbered mountains and with the Rogue River at its back door, Prospect retained strong traces of its rugged pioneer background, and this, combined with the comforts and amenities afforded by the gracious old hotel, made it as pleasant a place to linger for a week as most tourists could want.

During our first year at Prospect High, we occasionally encountered a likable youth known only as John. Although he was about a year older than Danny, John did not attend high school but was "bound out" by his parents in California to a rancher named Eldridge out on the splendid Red Blanket meadowland. His compensation consisted of board and room and a portion of the increase of the ranch in the form of a calf or shoat, which he was permitted to raise and market to provide meager funds for clothing and other necessities. Little was known about John, who volunteered few details about his background or circumstances; nevertheless, everyone liked the young bondsman and felt sympathy for his lonely and difficult situation.

One day John went fishing in the Rogue and failed to return in time for evening chores. A search party was organized under the leadership of Nelson Nye, son of old Chauncey Nye, the first settler to establish a home in the Upper Rogue River country back in post-Civil War days. Although Nelson Nye — one of the first whites born in southern Oregon — was in his late fifties at the time of this search, he was still regarded as the best tracker in Jackson County. The Prospect people knew he would need all his skill.

The days that followed produced conflicting reports. At school, we exchanged and amplified the latest rumors. John's fishing pole and hat had been recovered under a log jam. He had fallen off a cliff and dazedly staggered off in the wrong direction. He had fallen prey to a cougar or a bear. None of these possibilities seemed far-fetched to those who knew the country. Still the search pressed on, although as the days turned into weeks some members of the party were forced to give up and return to their normal duties.

Frank Ditsworth later recalled with awe the tenacity and cunning of Nelson Nye as he studied bent twigs and torn moss, noted clues, and circled in wide, carefully marked patterns. He ranged far from the river but always returned to its banks, steadily pursuing through the dense forest growth a thread so faint that the others began to suspect he was tracking only the phantoms of his imagination. At length, arriving at the lower end of Cascade Gorge, Nye separated from the party, crossed the river, and climbed to the rim of Red Rock Canyon while the others watched from below. High on the bluff, outlined against the sky, he paused and finally motioned the others to meet him downstream. Two hours later the party reassembled at our old Laurelhurst covered bridge.

"There's no use looking any more," Nye declared, studying the shale-surfaced road. "He's cleared out."

But the matter was not settled in the minds of the others, and conflicting reports continued to cloud the mystery of John's disappearance until it gradually gave way to more immediate concerns. A year went by. Then a startling but inconclusive report came out of the mountain town of Yreka in northern California, where a visiting Prospect lady had thought she recognized — and had even greeted — the missing lad, only to be answered by a stony stare as the youth she spoke to passed her in the street.

One day a letter came to Mrs. Pearson from an insurance company asking if she believed that John was still alive. The letter explained that the company was examining a claim submitted by John's mother, the beneficiary of a policy on his life. Mrs. Pearson, reflecting the division of the community, refused to venture an opinion either way. The claim was eventually paid, according to later reports.

The matter was resolved two years later when the Eldridges received a halting letter from John apologizing for all the trouble and anxiety he had caused them and others. The reason he gave for his action was homesickness and loneliness. But the facts suggest that the Great Depression and a conspiring mother also figured in the case.

chapter eleven
Exodus

OUR YEARS ON THE ROGUE rolled on like the river itself, each a
tributary different from the others in specific events but all
blending indistinguishably in the current of my memory. We
three boys were growing up and our parents were getting older.
The year was 1933 and — despite assurances from the new
president, Franklin Delano Roosevelt, that recovery was just
around the corner — the Depression prowled on like some tire-
less behemoth intent on devouring the entire nation.

Dad's hair was turning gray early, a common trait among the men in his family, and the natural reserve of his manner was hardening into a shell that even the family found difficult to penetrate. Although the old flashes of wit still gleamed at times, he seemed to find less occasion for humor than in our former years.

Mom continued to battle the Depression as a personal enemy, just as she did the balky woodstove. Her health problems were long behind her, and she was now a figure of strength and resolution. A firm believer in positive thinking and self-improvement, Mom regularly attended the county extension courses taught by Mabel Mack, who met with the ladies of the community and offered helpful tips on cutting corners and living on next to nothing. Still she found time to worry about the career prospects of her three growing sons. Many inconclusive conversations were held on this subject.

"Norm," she would begin in a purposeful tone that caused Dad to draw up his defenses. "What are we going to do when these boys grow up? If we stay here they will all become loggers. There's nothing else for them to do."

"What's the matter with logging?" Dad stalled. He knew perfectly well that logging ranked somewhere below bootlegging in Mom's hierarchy of occupational values. Detecting evasion, Mom's exasperation began to rise. She ignored the question.

"You had an education and they're entitled to their chance, too. I think we should go back to Medford where they can get some decent schooling and have a chance to do something besides cutting down trees and digging ditches."

Dad puffed his pipe for a time. Finally he said stiffly, "Well, I don't want them running the streets of Medford and getting into trouble."

This rejoinder, being too ludicrous to deserve a reply, received none and ended the discussion. Plainly, Dad was beginning to believe his old joke about Medford being "the wicked city."

But the matter would not rest there. Mom, the stubborn Norwegian, would not give up, nor would the three of us, who for reasons quite different from our mother's also yearned for the bright lights of city life. Danny, who was now driving the old Stevens and displaying an active interest in girls, needed a regular income to sustain his racy life style. I had achieved varsity status on the Prospect High basketball team and was looking for new and larger worlds to conquer. Bobby, two years my junior, had not yet exhibited the same restlessness, but soon his strong commercial inclinations would involve him in the general revolt. For the moment, however, our father's firm opposition thwarted all of these noble aspirations.

Then one day Mom stunned us with an altogether unexpected announcement. As we finished our supper and prepared to troop upstairs she informed us, a trifle awkwardly, that there would soon be another place at the table.

"Who's coming?" Bobby asked. "Relatives?"

Mom and Dad exchanged a conspiratorial smile. For a change, Dad's mood seemed less somber than it had been of late.

"Well, yes," said Mom; "but not the kind you are thinking about."

Our mouths fell open and for once we were at a loss for words. Danny was approaching sixteen, I was fourteen, and Bobby was twelve.

"You mean a baby?" Danny finally blurted out.

"That's right," Mom said, obviously pleased with herself at taking us so completely by surprise. Mom was then forty-two and, by our unenlightened reckoning, light-years beyond the proper — or biologically possible — age for childbearing. Up to that moment the possibility of any further increase in our family had no more entered our minds than had the prospect of entertaining a visitor from outer space.

From that moment this great coming event dominated our every waking thought and overshadowed all other considerations. The spare room was cleared and converted into a nursery. Dad set to work making a crib. We boys were at pains, for once, to spare our mother any undue effort.

Then, as the time drew nearer, Bobby began to act strangely quiet and thoughtful, almost worried. Noting his preoccupation, Mom asked what was bothering him. At first, Bobby didn't want to answer, but she questioned him persistently.

"Well, Mom," he said diffidently, "I saw some babies up at the mill without any clothes on. I hope we'll have enough money so our baby won't have to go naked."

Mom smiled gently. "I'm sure," she said, "that if God gives us this baby, he will see that it has clothes to wear."

For the time being the dolor of the Depression was relieved at our house by the prevailing mood of expectancy. Not a little of the excitement hinged on the question of the newcomer's sex. Another boy? Our parents looked at each other and paled. Surely, not another boy!

Ten days into the new year of 1934 a healthy, squalling baby girl arrived and settled all the speculation. She was christened Mary Ann and immediately became the center of all our attention. I don't know how our chores ever got done during the ensuing year. We fought for the privilege of holding and rocking her. Years later she said, "I didn't have any brothers; I had four fathers!"

Within the year following our sister's arrival, first Danny and then I, with Mom's connivance and help, made our way back into the larger world we had left behind eight years before. Danny obtained a bicycle delivery route (which later expanded into an automobile route) for the *Oregon Journal* newspaper. Mrs. Latham, mother of a large brood of her own and a friend and neighbor from our earlier Medford days, gave him board and room for a modest fee that left him with a few dollars for his personal needs. With this coup accomplished, Mom pressed on to resolve my situation. Throughout all this, Dad smoked his pipe and kept his own counsel.

We placed a classified advertisement in the Medford *Mail Tribune*, making known my availability for part-time work that would at least provide board and room. A response came sooner than expected when a well-dressed couple in a most unusual-looking automobile drove up to our gate. Sensing their purpose, I made haste to let them in, staring as I did so at the strange vehicle. It was a 1935 Chrysler Airflow, first of the Detroit experiments in aerodynamic streamlining, with the hood arching back from front bumper to windshield in a continuous sweeping curve.

The couple, Mr. and Mrs. Stewart of Medford, owned Adrienne's Dress Shop and needed janitorial services after store hours. Mr. Stewart — who seemed well satisfied with himself, his proud automobile, and his lovely wife — explained all this expansively.

Disregarding the fact that I had been identified as the applicant, he inspected the entire family carefully while continuing

100

to discuss his successful transition from Medford High School math teacher to retail businessman, as though his credentials rather than mine needed to be established. At length he pointed a plump finger at me and announced, "I'll take that one."

I suppose I should have been flattered, but it was with a sense of uneasiness and foreboding that I packed my few effects, said my goodbyes, and climbed into the fabulous Airflow.

Thus, quite abruptly, my part in the family's Rogue River saga came to an end save for those weekends when I was able to hitch rides home for overnight visits.

Within the year Bobby joined us in the wicked city. He also obtained a newspaper route, delivering the daily and Sunday *Tribune*, and like Danny found board and room with the Lathams. By this time Danny and I had each secured a second job after school hours (all three of us were now enrolled at Medford High), he as a general handyman at Hubbard Brothers' Hardware and I as part-time stock boy at Woolworth's.

Faced with the nearly forgotten responsibility of infant care and, shortly thereafter, the departure of their three half-grown sons, our parents found their situation drastically altered. Most of the consequences devolved upon Mom, for Dad's dignity precluded his involvement in domestic duties. In any case, he was frequently away from home on county and federal jobs, which by this time were becoming somewhat more regularly available. So our mother, who had put herself into this fix by her complicity in our leave-taking, had to work twice as hard as formerly and devise many desperate stratagems to accomplish all the work that was thus dumped upon her.

Many of her activities forced her to be away from the house for short periods, and she took to combining these tasks so that her absences gradually increased to as much as half an hour at a time. Each time she returned to find the baby sleeping or playing happily in her crib, so Mom began to feel reasonably comfortable with this practice. The months slipped by, and somehow our parents managed to do all that was required of them.

Perhaps once or twice a month we were able to be home together for a weekend. We rejoiced in these brief family reunions and spoiled Mary Ann outrageously. Never had the little "chalet" seemed so warm and hospitable nor the surrounding green hills so lovely. Sometimes we managed to get together with the other young people at the Glass ranch for a hike, a baseball game, or a singalong. Then, all too soon, it was late Sunday afternoon and time to thumb a ride back to Medford.

Suddenly it was 1936. President Roosevelt easily won reelection over the earnest Kansan, Alf Landon, on the basis of his demonstrated concern for the economic ills of the nation, but the Depression still clawed at the land.

Mary Ann was a bright, inquisitive toddler of two and had learned by hard experience to avoid such dangers as the open stairwell. Dad was sometimes away for weeks at a time, and Mom continued to try to be in several places at once. To compensate, and to provide companionship for Mary Ann, Dad found a cute mongrel puppy at the county dog pound. For once, Dad didn't strain for a high-sounding name but simply called the dog Dizzy. The two little ones immediately became inseparable.

One day Mom hurried back to the house after dispatching a handful of chores and looked in on the nursery. The baby was nowhere to be found. Dizzy was also missing. With growing uneasiness, she searched first the house, then the outbuildings and the surrounding yard, calling both the child and the puppy by name. There was no answer.

For the first time in her ten years on the Rogue, Mom felt real terror. Through her mind flashed all the perils we had survived during those years — rattlesnakes, runaway horses, the river . . . the river! She raced down the hill and across the flat. Obeying some impulse, she went directly to the nearest point on the bank, which happened to be our family picnic ground. There at the water's edge she found the two little wanderers.

Mary Ann looked up in sweet unconcern at her mother's distraught face.

"Dizzy thirsty," she explained calmly.

That, of course, put an end to the Rogue River adventure. Mom notified our father straightaway that she was taking the baby and returning to Medford with or without him. She would leave as soon as she could find a place to live. Dad made no protest. He loved his little daughter as much as any father ever loved his child, and the experience had shaken him as badly as it had our mother. Furthermore, it was apparent that Mom meant business. He set about to make the necessary arrangements.

It must have been a bitter defeat for Dad, although, characteristically, he concealed his deep disappointment. For ten years he had held on to an impossible dream. None of his wild schemes had materialized despite sometimes heroic struggles against the odds. His sons had forsaken the old squirrel ranch in favor of the wicked city and his gallant partner was breathing threats of mutiny.

Dad was a resourceful and visionary man but, despite his colorful way with words, a poor communicator. None of us, including Mom, ever really understood what was in his mind or what dreams lured him on. In retrospect, I think the most painful aspect of retreat for him was the certainty that his treasured river land, which he was forced to sacrifice for less than he paid, would eventually appreciate many times over in value. So events proved, at any rate. Heavily mortgaged as it was, the place barely brought us enough to start anew in the most meager of circumstances. In the years that followed, the property changed hands a number of times and was owned for a period by the actor and later U.S. senator George Murphy, who raised hogs there.

In the end, the entire Laurelhurst district was condemned and purchased by the federal government for a thousand dollars an acre. Thus, in a generation, the land we had clung to so precariously for a decade appreciated seventy-fold, whereas we barely got out with our skins intact.

Once the painful decision was made, Dad accomplished the relocation swiftly. He found employment with an old friend, Scott Brill, who operated a sheet-metal shop in the building formerly occupied by Dad's old Vulcan Welding Works. Next, he rented a small, drafty house on West Jackson Street. We boys returned to the family circle and, in this dreary crackerbox, endured one of the coldest winters of my life. In the spring Dad was able to move the family to a more suitable dwelling, an old farmhouse with small acreage on Buckshot Hill north of town. There we began to pick up again the threads of urban life.

chapter twelve
Return to the river

AFTER OUR FAMILY returned to Medford we saw very little of the old Laurelhurst district or its people. One fall Dad and I went hunting there, and I shot a spike buck at the crest of Jim Mann Hill above our old house. Other than that, I remember no contact with our old neighborhood. Within a few years our family left the Rogue River Valley.

I was first to go, a victim of the chronically blighted regional economy, which still stubbornly rejected the medication being applied successfully elsewhere to the Depression malady. A year at the University of Oregon had exhausted my savings; another year of continuous unemployment forced me to make a hard decision. I borrowed enough money to get to Southern California and wait out a job in the burgeoning aircraft industry. It was 1939, and our country was beginning to produce lend-lease warplanes for France and Britain.

The following year our parents moved to Bremerton, Washington, where the government shipyard was going stronger than it had since World War I. Dad bought a run-down cabin court and turned his versatility to the task of converting decrepit cottages into suitable dwellings for the influx of defense workers and their families. My two brothers soon joined the family: Bob operated a cleaning establishment and Dan got a job as a milkman. Before long I too came to Washington and found employment at the Boeing plant in Seattle.

Within another year the nation was at war and the three of us had enlisted in the Army Air Corps. Soon we were scattered across the country and moving rapidly from one training center to another. At the war's end Dan and I settled in the state of Washington, but Bob remained in the service and made a career of flying jets.

The years have flown by. Our contacts with the old community on the Upper Rogue have been infrequent and sketchy, mostly brief stopovers or Christmas card exchanges with old friends.

I remember that the Christmas news in 1955 was bleak. During the preceding week the Rogue had gone on one of its famous rampages, bringing destruction far greater than the flood of 1927 that marked our arrival. This was not so much because of higher water (the two floods were fairly equal in volume and duration) but because there was a great deal more property to be destroyed by 1955.

The reaction to this new disaster was greatly different from the meek acceptance of earlier flood victims. The advance of technology, the rise in affluence, and the sense of having more to lose had produced a combative spirit in many southern Oregonians. Flood control dams were appearing in other parts of the country, they noted; why not in the Rogue River Valley? Militant

civic leaders like Ben Hilton of Grants Pass began making overtures to the federal government. The Corps of Engineers was
asked to look into the problem.

After a lengthy series of surveys the Corps assured the valley
folk that a system of dams would, indeed, remove the danger of
future floods. Of course, some land would have to be sacrificed,
and Congress would have to be persuaded to vote a considerable
appropriation, but these were not insurmountable obstacles if
the will of the people was solidly behind the idea.

But the will of the people, it soon turned out, was by no means
unanimous. Friends of the river, who loved the wild Rogue in all
its moods, quickly became aroused. Dam the Rogue? Monstrous!
Indignation meetings were held and letters, pro and con, were
fired off to congressmen and editors. Clearly, the threat of a dam
was real this time and no longer some visionary technocrat's
dream. A high dam on the Upper Rogue was not only possible
but, in view of the new mood of the property owners, distinctly
probable.

The old-timers were generally neutral, neither sentimental
about the river nor particularly hostile toward it. They had seen
its wild force — some had even lost loved ones as well as
precious acres and toil-won houses — but they had known
these risks when they established their homestead claims.

"They call it the Rogue, don't they?" said old Frank Ditsworth
dryly.

The issue was finally settled in October 1962 when Congress
voted to authorize the project. The plan called for construction
of three dams. At the proposed Lost Creek site, just above our old
place, a rock and gravel dam would rise 360 feet and back water
up six miles to the lower end of Cascade Gorge, effectively
obliterating the neighborhood in which I grew up. A few miles
downstream another dam of similar material, 235 feet high, was
to be located at Elk Creek, a tributary of the Rogue. This edifice
was destined to flood more than a hundred thousand primitive
acres. And in the high Siskiyous, near the California border, the
beautiful upper Applegate River was to be subdued by a 230-foot
earthen dam near the mountain town of Copper. The entire
project was then estimated to cost about $200 million.

Over the years, I recalled with increasing frequency the precious events of our Rogue River experience. These I shared with

my children, first Laurie and then, eight years later, Stephen. "Oregon stories" became a bedtime ritual; the more exciting episodes had to be retold many times as my supply of such reminiscences ran low. A special favorite was the Lost Creek trip described in chapter nine. Betty, my wife, has been forced to listen to the saga of Lost Creek many times.

Stimulated by an appreciative audience in the person of Laurie (Steve was then just on the way) — and perhaps prodded by Dad's death in 1963 — I discovered that these recollections were arousing a powerful desire to revisit my old haunts. At length, in the summer of 1964, I persuaded the family that we should spend our vacation in southern Oregon. As the time of our departure approached, my sense of expectancy became tinged with foreboding, for the speculation about a dam on the Upper Rogue had advanced well beyond the rumor stage. I was aware that the location most frequently mentioned for its erection was the mouth of Lost Creek.

Our first stop was at the old family home. The scene was scarcely recognizable. Both barns and the original trees were gone, and the "chalet" had undergone so many additions and renovations that no one would have connected it even remotely with its former architecture. My strongest impression of the surrounding scene was of a great deal of white board fencing.

The middle-aged gentleman who answered our knock was courteous but not effusive. We exchanged introductions and I learned that he was a retired Army colonel now raising purebred horses. He seemed not overly impressed by the news that I had grown up in his present domicile but consented to allow us to cross his property on foot, subject to elaborate instructions about closing gates, not disturbing a new foal, and so on. Betty, who was then in the eighth month of her pregnancy with Steve, waited in the car for Laurie and me.

Our hike beside the well-remembered river turned out to be a disappointing experience for me. Gone were the islands and the swimming hole, ripped out by the 1955 flood, which left the bank as raw and straight as a levee. Gone also was Dad's old irrigation reservoir, and I couldn't find even a trace of Bobby Creek. We did, however, surprise a doe on the upper flat near the scene of our many nocturnal hunts, confirming the observation that deer continue to use their ancestral paths through countless generations. I returned to the car feeling vaguely dissatisfied but still hopeful as we continued our tour.

My hopes brightened when I found the Laurelhurst Loop road relatively unchanged from my boyhood days. Nearly forgotten landmarks appeared, seeming to welcome me home. The stately oaks on the meadow of the old Train place were much larger and nobler than I remembered them. The old Brophy schoolhouse, predating even our ancient Laurelhurst school, was recognizable, though it now served as a residence and was surrounded by delapidated cars and trucks. Eagerly, I began looking for Lost Creek.

Then, abruptly, I found it. But the road, instead of looping through tall trees as I remembered, opened onto an obviously new section — wide, straight, and elevated by a dike of coarse aggregate fill. The dense giant trees I remembered were mostly gone; the smaller evergreens remaining were scraggly and scarred as though by heavy machinery. Reddish, murky water coursed through a silt-laden channel and puked out of a culvert on the downhill side of the road. A new, gravel-surfaced road wound up the mountainside. I turned onto it numbly, dreading what I might discover next.

Three quarters of a mile up the road, on a slope now laid waste by clearcut logging, we arrived at a point where, I sensed, the falls of Lost Creek should be if any sanity or stability remained in southern Oregon. Leaving Betty and Laurie in the car, I scrambled down a muddy bank barricaded in many places by jumbles of rejected logs and tangled mounds of forest trash. Like a distraught parent searching for a child in some terrible jungle, I kept looking for the falls.

At the bottom of the ravine I found Lost Creek, winding sluggishly through its silted channel, but there was no sign of a sylvan falls, nor any possibility of one remaining in that chaos. I climbed slowly back up the muddy bank. Doggedly I drove on up the scarred and barren hill, gripped by some nameless need to confirm what I did not want to know.

Presently we came to a parked Army vehicle with the insignia of the Corps of Engineers emblazoned on its door. Several young men in green fatigues were fixing grade stakes by the roadside. They stared impassively as I stopped, got out, and greeted them.

"What's the Army doing up here?" I asked, trying to sound

properly friendly and not too inquisitive.

The noncom in charge of the group took his time answering while he measured me with a cool glance.

"Just surveying," he responded briefly.

Sensing that nothing more would come of the conversation, I nodded and left. At the bottom of the hill I turned north on the Laurelhurst road and carefully avoided looking back at Lost Creek.

One objective of this vacation trip was to satisfy Mom's curiosity concerning our old neighbor Stewart Weeks, orchardist and — as Dad had sometimes called him — "squire of Laurelhurst." Aside from Mom's interest, I also looked forward to this reunion with a highly respected figure from my past.

After his mother died, Stewart Weeks had elected to live on alone in the family log cabin, which was deep in a stand of giant Douglas firs. As boys, we had been fascinated by this rustic home and its primeval setting, which even then had seemed anachronistic. There was about the place a forbidding air of gloom and isolation. I thought it strange that a well-to-do man would choose to live alone in such bleak surroundings.

As though to confirm these thoughts, there had been disturbing reports over the years about changes in the life and personality of the dignified bachelor. It was said that a woman had set a snare for him but had succeeded only in ruining his health and polluting his simple style of living. Finally accepting that he would never marry her, she had abandoned him to alcoholism and eccentricity. He had lived on alone in the old cabin, ignoring mail, seeing few of his neighbors, and even refusing to pay his taxes. Logging operators had urged him for years to permit selective cutting of the firs, which would only grow diseased and unsafe with age, but he refused, vowing to preserve the property in its natural state to honor the memory of his father and grandfather.

One day Frank Ditsworth had gone to see Weeks on some business matter. He found the hired man puttering about the old packing house.

"Stew Weeks around?" Frank asked.

"Up in the cabin, I guess," the overseer responded.

"How long since you've seen him?"

"Couple of weeks."

"Two weeks!" Frank exclaimed. "He could be dead!"

"Yeah," the hired man smirked. "Dead drunk."

Ditsworth found his neighbor in a sodden stupor and the cabin in hideous disarray. Reports of incidents like this one were on my mind as I turned into the narrow road through the tall trees.

The old log cabin was much as I remembered it, except visibly run down. At my knock, a decrepit ruin of an old man came to the door. Mr. Weeks didn't invite us in but leaned shakily against the corner of the house during our brief conversation. Red veins coursed his pouched cheeks, and his watery eyes spoke of infinite sadness and pain, yet a trace of the old courtliness remained in his words and manner.

"Certainly I recall your family," he said. "I remember the twinkle in your father's eye. He was a grand man. And your mother; how is she?"

He smiled wanly when I asked about the orchard. He said that the trees had grown old, like himself, and had finally fallen prey to the diseases his grandfather had sought to avoid. Also, the only available labor in later times was provided by Mexican migrant workers, who did not always want to journey so far from the major agricultural areas. He had finally closed down, just a couple of years previously.

As we shook hands in parting, he smiled again. "You look like your dad. Don't lose that twinkle in your eye."

Six months after this trip another pre-Christmas flood ripped through the Rogue River Valley. Statewide, Oregon experienced an estimated billion dollars worth of flood damage in December 1964, and the worst of this was in the southwest corner of the state. This time the devastation on the Upper Rogue was appalling. Below the picturesque old Laurelhurst covered bridge, a huge slide swept away much of the slope extending down to the river from the old Weeks and Ditsworth properties. Downstream, Casey State Park (once Casey's campground) lay buried under debris, and our beloved old McLeod bridge had simply disappeared, leaving only its scarred and graffiti-covered concrete abutments looming as monuments to the past. Many stretches of the Crater Lake Highway had also vanished, especially those nearest the river.

Whatever opposition still delayed initiation of the Rogue Basin Flood Control Project was also swept away by this most terrible of all floods on the Rogue. Contracts were quickly let and preparations made for the construction of the three federal dams: Lost Creek (on the Rogue), Elk Creek (a tributary seven or eight miles downstream),* and the Applegate River to the south.

Work began at Lost Creek in 1966. Gigantic yellow machines crawled the river bed like grotesquely magnified crayfish, scouring gravel pockets, rerouting the channel, and nudging aside boulder, bridge, and island. Ashore, bulldozers and earth movers pawed at forest and field. Dynamite blasts tore out whole hillsides and leveled stands of virgin Douglas fir. Some of the better houses were moved to other sites by rigs that negotiated the narrow river road beneath the overhanging cliffs with infinite skill and patience. Cabins, shacks, and barns were pushed into splintered heaps to be burned along with tree stumps and brush.

Construction of the Lost Creek Dam, like other phases of the Rogue's history, did not go unmarked by tragedy. One day a quality control manager for one of the contractors went looking for some friends who were salvaging materials from the old Weeks packing house. (By that time Stew Weeks had been dead for several years.) He drove into the deserted ranch, stripped of both pear and fir trees, and headed toward the old packing shed, still being emptied of equipment. He assumed that his friends were eating lunch there. A wire dangled from a crazily leaning pole, blocking his path. Thinking it only a telephone line connecting the many and widely dispersed dam site operations, he reached out to brush it aside and was electrocuted. It was later learned that the pole had been knocked askew by a backhoe. The driver of the backhoe, who had also mistaken the wire for a telephone line, had not bothered to report the incident.

The forebodings that had haunted me from my earliest awareness of the proposed flood control project could not allay my interest in, or curiosity about, its progress. In mid-October 1973, Betty and I took Steve, now a husky nine-year-old, for a long weekend visit to southern Oregon. Leaving the freeway at Cottage Grove, we drove south by the Diamond Lake route,

---

*The Elk Creek Project was cancelled in 1976 as a result of opposition from environmentalist and conservation groups.

111

where a trace of new snow mantled the spindly lodgepole pines. I told Steve again about the time I rowed the five-mile length of this lake and back, when I was about his age, and he was duly impressed by the lake's considerable expanse. We stopped for a bite of lunch at Union Creek, then drove on to Prospect, where my brothers and I had attended high school.

On the surface, Prospect looked much like the little mountain town I remembered from the thirties. School kids on their lunch hour thronged the old log store just as we had done. The school buildings and grounds seemed little changed except for the growth of the fir tree standing across the walk from the store drinking fountain. The old Prospect Hotel was deteriorating, however. The roof sagged and tall grass and unpruned shrubbery choked the yard. We learned that Jim Grieve, the jovial hosteler of my youth, had been dead for some years, but Heston, his younger brother, made an appearance and seemed genuinely pleased to see me again. He invited us to tour the hotel, which now bore a hand-lettered sign, "Dewey Hill, Prop." Steve's eyes popped at the splendid array of pelts, heads, and antlers of animals adorning the peeling walls. Betty was enchanted by the kitchen with its enormous old woodburning cookstove that had for nearly a century produced meals for tourists, dignitaries, and lumberjacks and still showed signs of regular use.

Behind the hotel the moss-covered cabins were sinking into ruin, though a few still showed evidence of occupancy. A clutter of old car parts and other refuse littered the ground under the big trees.

I prowled the grounds with Steve until eventually we came upon the person I was looking for: a rawboned old man in a yellow sweatshirt and baseball cap. He stared at us through eyes grown dim since I had seen them last.

"Want to wrestle, Dewey?" I asked, grasping the veined and bony old hand.

He responded with a perfunctory echo of the old bravado, but I could see that he didn't know me, so I introduced myself.

"Oh, yeah, the Ohrt boys. From down by McLeod." A brief flicker of interest enlivened his countenance. It was evident that his eyesight was nearly gone.

"Dewey, this is my boy Steve. Think he'll make a ball player?"

Dewey took young Steve's hand in his. He treated the question quite seriously and seemed to frame his assessment through touch rather than sight. "Kinda small," he muttered vaguely. "Might make it, though."

We drove out onto the Red Blanket, that once-primitive meadow that, even as late as my high school years, had evoked in my imagination the ghosts of Indians and frontiersmen. A dusty road now wound through a jumble of cottages and shacks surrounded by pickups, logging trucks, motorcycles, boats, campers, trailers, and snowmobiles. Around us, the jutting mountains plainly showed the ravages of clearcut logging, but on a fine day such as this their beauty still dazzled the eye.

Returning through town as we prepared to leave Prospect on our way south, I got out of the car to snap another picture or two. On the hotel porch a gaunt figure in a yellow sweatshirt sat hunched and motionless. The stained baseball cap was pulled low over the hooded eyes.

"So long, Dewey," I called, waving. But I got no reply. Perhaps he was napping, dreaming in the fall sunshine of glories long ago.

A few minutes after leaving Prospect we turned off the Crater Lake Highway and onto a blacktop parking lot near where a sign proclaimed, "Observation Point — Lost Creek Dam Construction Project." Soon we were looking down upon a scene of swarming activity that bore no resemblance to my boyhood home. Directly below us the footings of the dam were taking shape at a point quite near where Danny and I had alternated at "walking the ditch" on hot summer days. Upstream, mountains of gravel and broad expanses of raw, bulldozed earth replaced what once had been the Train, Brophy, Weeks, and Ditsworth properties. Trucks rumbled to and fro, and whistles tooted peremptory signals to drivers and work crews.

Threading through this scene, the once wild, rebellious, and unconquerable Rogue coursed its way meekly between the banks of a manmade channel. From where we stood it looked for all the world like an oversized irrigation ditch.

A mile or so downstream lay the river flat at the foot of the hill where once had perched our "chalet" — it, too, had disappeared, along with all its tacked-on additions. On this river flat we had picked mushrooms after the spring rains and hazelnuts in the fall, floated "pummey rocks" in the current, and launched our Roman candles on the Fourth of July. Here I had hunted rabbits and dreamed away timeless, sun-drenched hours. Here Dad had envisioned the trout farm that would make our fortunes.

Through the swirling mist of the late October afternoon I could make out a series of long, narrow rectangles of concrete clustered at the site where Dad had planned to put his trout ponds. They were the rearing ponds of the federally funded Cole Rivers Fish Hatchery. Its purpose, according to the legend in the observation room, was to replace the natural spawning beds of salmon and steelhead, now permanently displaced by the dam.

Across the meticulous diagram of the dam and hatchery, someone had scrawled a grease pencil message on the glass cover.

"Death to the river!"

"Let's go," I said.